HEIRLOOM KNITTING FOR DOLLS

HEIRLOOM KNITTING FOR DOLLS

Classic Patterns in Knitted Cotton

Furze Hewitt

Photography by Robert Roach
Line illustrations by Josephine Hoggan

ROBERT HALE • LONDON

To my children
and
their children

Acknowledgments

My grateful thanks to Robert Roach for his exceptional skill as a photographer of white lace knitting.

A special thankyou to the following: Edna Lomas for her skill in knitting dolls' clothes. Kathy Grin for creating Klasina. To the doll creators, Patricia Blyth, Ellen Watt, Ria Warke, Kaye Wiggs and Aileen Sellen. Ria Warke for the use of her antique prams, James Botham for lending his antique brass bed and Nora, his antique A.M. 370 doll, Keith Hewitt for restoring the miniature furniture, Gillian Colquhoun for once again typing the manuscript, Jane Cottee for her help with the sets at Cockington Green, and proof reading, James and Robert Colquhoun for their help in checking the manuscript, to my friend Carol Davey for the use of her collection of the odd and interesting, John Cummins of Queanbeyan Books and Prints for his diligent search for knitting patterns, Josephine Hoggan for her charming drawings, Thea Moore for her advice on the doll world, and her sewing skills, John Miller, Manager of Cockington Green, for his permission to use the Miniature Village, and also at Cockington Green, Ray Jones, Train Driver, for his cooperation.

The following have helped in various ways: Clair and Jessica Chute, Carol Coates, Jos Csibi, Glennis Ayres, Patsy Ranger, Maurine Rogers, Roslyn Panetta, Judith Mansfield, Victoria Clark, Don Macleod, Rina and Dina Tagliapietra, Michael and Paula Roath, Barbara Hosking, Ruth Rintoule, Val Cooper, Jo Waring, Joan Eckersley, Ann Dalton, Pat Walsh, Patricia Wain, Elizabeth Nugent, Barbara Wild, Bronwyn Coote, Anna Sliwinski, Glyn Hopson, Lesley Rowe, Wendy Loftus and June Witt.

Special thanks to Lorraine Kiewiets of Annie's Cakes, Crawford Centre, Queanbeyan. Lorraine made, and donated, the delightful flower arrangement in Dolly Pentreath's photograph.

My grateful thanks to everyone who make this book possible.

First published in Great Britain in 1993
Paperback edition 1994

ISBN-0-7090-5560-9

Robert Hale Limited
Clerkenwell House
Clerkenwell Green
London EC1R 0HT

Printed in Hong Kong by Colorcraft Ltd

Contents

Kate, dressed in nineteenth century broderie anglaise, escorts Dolly Pentreath (page 51) to visit Cockington Green.

Foreword

As a dollmaker and teacher of dollmaking I am constantly in touch with other dollmakers and I know their problems.

One of the major problems, encountered almost every day, is the inability to get dolls dressed. And there are as many excuses for this as there are naked dolls. 'Can't find the time,' some say. 'Can't sew,' others admit. 'Don't know where to begin' is another excuse.

But I don't think I have ever heard anyone confess to being unable to knit. After all, there are only two stitches to master but the ways those stitches can be organised and utilised to produce a finished article never fails to amaze.

An added advantage of knitting is that it can be done at almost any time. You can't carry your sewing machine in your handbag but you can carry your knitting and get on with it during a ten-minute relaxation in the park after lunch. You can knit during friendly coffee breaks, while watching television and on the hundred and one other occasions during the course of a day when the hands are idle.

Therefore when someone with a love of dolls and a love of knitting decides to combine the two loves it's a big occasion and a great opportunity for many aspiring doll dressers. Furze Hewitt has created the occasion and provided the opportunity in this marvellous book that cannot fail to bring greater colour into the lives of dollmakers.

But there is more to the book than knitting. The pictures with the dolls shown in tableau situations could well lead to a new and exciting method of doll presentation and display.

Pat Blyth, Master Dollmaker

Shopping for knitted lace at Second-Hand Rose.

Introduction

The collecting and crafting of porcelain dolls is steadily increasing. Dollmakers worldwide are endeavouring to capture the beauty of antique dolls, and to create original modern dolls.

Dressmaking for dolls requires infinite patience and skill. This book of heirloom knitting for dolls is intended to be an alternative to dressmaking. The designs are simple and charming—the work portable and rewarding.

Happy knitting.

Generous quantities of thread are given with each pattern; this will enable you to create your own version of the design, using your preference in skirt length, and maybe adding a hat, without the worry of running out of cotton. Care should be taken to purchase your cotton from the same dye lot. Buy an extra ball if you are unsure of your requirements.

The materials you use should be the finest available. The small amount of thread required to dress a doll makes it worthwhile. Using a quality thread, the lace will be clearer, and the design crisp. Inferior cotton has a tendency to obscure the lace holes, destroying the clarity of the pattern.

Use cotton thread when attaching lace, or sewing fine seams. Synthetic threads can cut fine fabrics, and they have a tendency to yellow with age.

Use fine silk thread to sew silk ribbons, silk fabric or silk knitting.

Silk ribbons are effective in trimming fine cotton lace. The delicate sheen of the silk complements the soft sheen of mercerised cotton thread. Silk ribbons are readily available, and come in a range of subtle colours, making them ideal to trim your heirloom knitting. For thicker cotton knitting, try lengths of finely knitted cord—you will find a pattern in the trims. Avoid the use of satin

or synthetic ribbons. Keep decorative trims on the knitted garments to a minimum, allowing the simple beauty of cotton knitting to enhance the charm of your doll.

Knitting needles are now available in the smaller sizes. We no longer have to resort to hat pins and darning needles to create fine knitting. Treat these tiny needles with the care they deserve, both in use and storage.

Stockists of fine yarns and needles are listed at the back of the book for your convenience.

Cotton and its care

Cotton is a natural fibre, made from the long filaments of the cotton boll.

The use of white cotton was at its peak in the Victorian era. During this period there was a craze for white cotton knitting. It was used to trim household and personal linen. The lace, and the tiny garments in this book, were knitted in white. Today the cotton is available in a wide range of colours, including unusual dyes, suitable for trimming heirloom knitting. Dolly Pentreath's dress flounce, collar and cuffs were knitted in a warm cinnamon shade—a rich contrast, perfect with the black moiré dress. Ask to see the shade chart at your yarn shop. The use of colour can enhance your doll. Knitting in white has the advantage, of course, that colour can be introduced in ribbons and accessories.

Cotton is an easy care fibre

It is safest to hand wash your dolls' clothes. Turn the garment inside out to protect the surface of the knitted fabric from wear. Do not rub stains, but squeeze gently under the water to loosen soiled areas. Rinse in the same temperature water that you used for the washing. Roll the garment in a towel to remove excess moisture. Place the knitting on a flat surface and gently pull into shape, taking care not to stretch the ribbing. Leave to dry naturally.

Never hang a knitted garment on the line. Cotton knitting responds to a light pressing. Use a towel underneath the knitting to prevent the design from being flattened. Ribbed or pleated knitting should not be pressed. Some articles, such as fine laces, benefit from a light spray of starch.

Storing dolls and dolls' clothes

Wrap dolls and garments in clean soft sheeting or acid-free paper. Do not use plastic or cardboard containers. The use of plastic can cause a build-up of moisture, while the chemicals used in the production of cardboard can cause fabrics to deteriorate.

If you need to store dolls or clothes for a long time, use aromatic sachets to dispel moths, and to give the stored articles an old world fragrance.

Notes on the designs

The edgings, braids and beadings in this book are from the white knitting era of a century ago. These tiny edgings, often only a few stitches, are ideal for the novice lace knitter, or for those knitters whose hands are no longer strong enough to cope with full size garments. The wider laces take less time to make than traditional pillow or needle laces. You can knit delicate lace at a fraction of the cost of machine made lace.

Hats are often a problem in knitting. Designs for berets, hoods and bonnets can be found quite readily, but these can be limiting when dressing an antique doll. The bobble bonnet is the perfect answer. You can tie the curtain back with a bow, or let it hang, to form a cape. Rosie and Nora show how effective the bonnet can be. You can make the bonnet without its curtain. (The term 'curtain' is often used in Victorian hood and bonnet patterns, probably because it forms a screen around the neck or shoulders.)

I have designed a simple Granny bonnet in a luxury yarn, knitted in black for Dolly Pentreath, a pearly grey for Thea, and a persimmon shade for the bonnet in the shop scene. One ball of Gyps'Anny from the Anny Blatt range was sufficient for each bonnet. The texture of the knitting felt like fine straw, very suitable for a hat. The design of the Granny bonnet is so basic even a child could make it. Using different yarns and trims, your doll can wear a hat that you have created.

Even a cheap woven straw hat can be trimmed to enhance your doll. The one Sarah is wearing (page 55) has a tiny lace edging knitted on size 20 needles. The hatband is a knitted length of Launceston lace. The addition of a length of antique ribbon makes the hat interesting. The hat complements her simple muslin dress and was created at little cost.

Trims have been included amongst the patterns—not only are they economical, they provide the type of embellishment knitting requires. Leave the machine-made laces, instant trims, rosettes, etc. to the non-knitters.

Knitted garments *need* knitted lace—it has the same texture so it blends perfectly with the rest of the garment.

The beds in the book rely on fine threads and needles for their appeal. Time, of course, was also necessary to create the hangings and bedding. Why not dress a bed for your doll or your favourite charity?

Most of the patterns date from the middle of the nineteenth century. They came to me from many sources, in several countries. I am grateful for the generosity of the knitters who shared their families' treasured patterns. *Heirloom Knitting for Dolls* preserves these often tattered instructions for future generations to enjoy.

I have enjoyed my contact with the world of dolls. I hope you, the lace knitter, will use the book we have created to increase your knowledge and skills in the gentle craft of lace knitting.

Abbreviations and Terms

Abbreviations are used in knitting instructions to save space, and to make the pattern easier to follow. It is important to read, and understand, the abbreviations before beginning to knit a pattern.

In this book most of the patterns use standard British abbreviations.

In ordinary knitting the made sts consist of the following:

yfwd   between two knit stitches
yon   between a purl and knit action
yrn   between two purl actions

In this book the above actions are referred to as m1—make one, as they are commonly written in old lace patterns.

Some helpful abbreviations

k	knit
p	purl
st	stitch
sts	stitches
b	back
f	front
sl	slip
wyib	with yarn in back
wyif	with yarn in front
tog	together
*m1	make one stitch by winding yarn round needle
turn	work is turned before end of row
dpn	double pointed needle
motif	design unit
st st	stocking stitch—knit right side, purl wrong side
garter st	knit all rows
mb	make bobble
beg	beginning
psso	pass slipped stitch over
p2sso	pass 2 slipped stitches over
p-wise	purlwise
k-wise	knitwise

*In old knitting publications the increase in lace knitting was referred to in several different ways: o—over; m1—make one; and cast up.

tbl	through back of loop
ybk	yarn back
yfwd	yarn forward
yon	yarn over needle
yrn	yarn around needle
R.H.	right hand
L.H.	left hand
tw st	twist stitch
inc	increase
dc	double crochet
ch	chain

Comparative terms

British	American
cast off	bind off
tension	gauge
alternate rows	every other row
miss	skip
work straight	work even
stocking stitch	stockinette stitch
shape cap	shape top

Knitting needle sizes

Metric	British	American
2mm	14	00
2¼	13	0
2¾	12	1
3	11	2
3¼	10	3
3¾	9	4
4	8	5
4½	7	6
5	6	7
5½	5	8
6	4	9
6½	3	10
7	2	10½
7½	1	11
8	0	12
9	00	13
10	000	15

Techniques

Casting on

Step 1

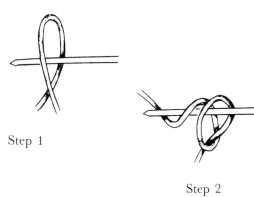

Step 2

Step 3

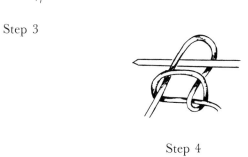

Step 4

Thumb method of casting on

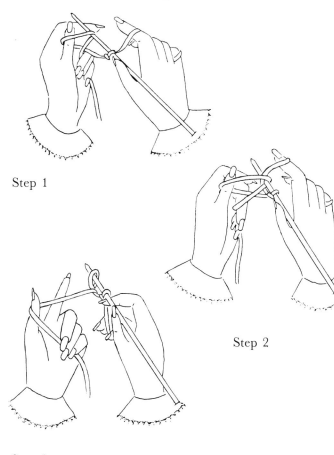

Step 1

Step 2

Step 3

How to knit

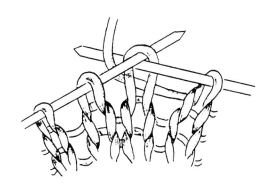

How to purl

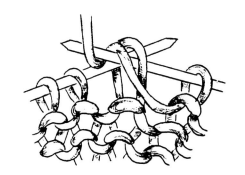

Invisible cast on method
1. Using contrasting thread, cast on the number of stitches required, work two rows in stocking stitch.
2. With main thread, continue work until length required.
3. When work is completed, remove contrasting thread. Either graft or sew together open stitches from both ends of work.

Fig. 2

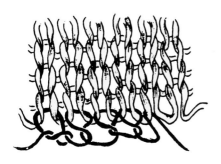

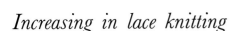
Increasing in lace knitting

There are three methods of increasing the number of stitches on a row, or in a round. One way is to knit twice into a stitch (Fig. 1). This increase can be worked k-wise or p-wise. Read your pattern carefully and work as directed.

A second method is to pick up a loop between two sts, and knit into that loop (Fig. 2). This prevents a hole forming in the knitting.

The third method (Fig. 3), make one (or m1), produces the holes in lace knitting. The way it is worked depends on whether the extra stitch is to be made between two knit stitches, a knit and a purl, or two purl stitches. Between knit sts the yarn is brought forward, and over the needle as you knit the next stitch, thus forming a new stitch. Once again, read your pattern carefully.

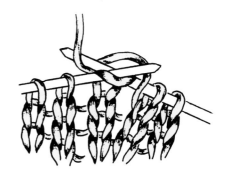

Fig. 3

(a) Make one between two knit stitches

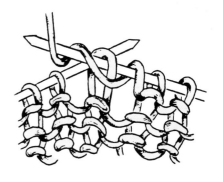

(b) Make one between two purl stitches

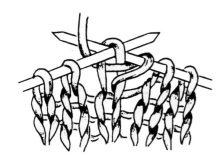

Fig. 1

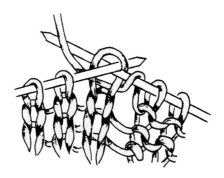

(c) Make one between a knit and a purl stitch

Decreasing in lace knitting

Again there are several methods. One method is to knit or purl two stitches together (Fig. 4a and b). A second method is to pass the next but one stitch previously worked over the latter (Fig. 4c and d).

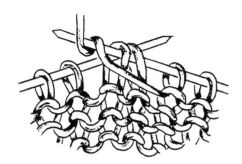

Fig. 4 (a)

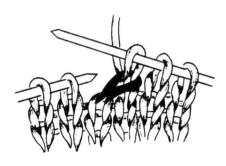

(b)

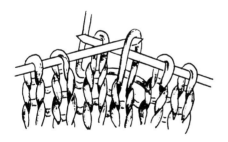

(c)

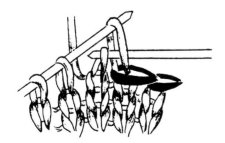

(d)

Knitted picot cast off

Knit 1st st. *Sl 1 st from R.H. needle on to L.H. needle. Insert needle into this st, cast on 2 sts, then cast off 5 sts. Repeat from * until all sts have been cast off.

Knitting off your stitches if you can't crochet

K1, *k2 tog, m1, k2 tog, turn. P1, *(k1, p1) twice, k1 * in next st.
P1, sl 1 purlwise, turn. Cast off 7 sts (1 st left on R.H. needle)*.
Repeat from *-* to last 5 sts. K3 tog, m1, k2 tog, turn, p1 (k1, p1) twice, k1, in next st, p1, sl 1, purlwise, turn. Cast off remaining sts.
For a larger loop on your edging, make 9 sts instead of the 5 sts described above.

THE PATTERNS

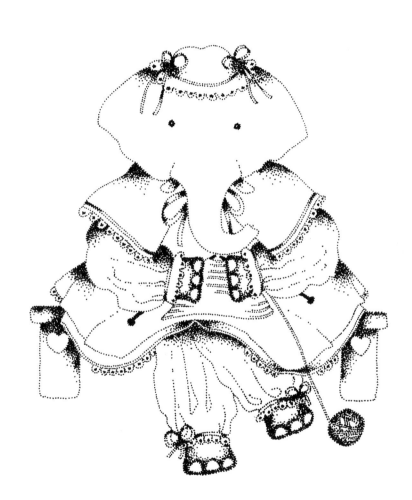

Dress: GLYN

Reproduction long-faced Jumeau 18'' (46 cm).
Doll is wearing a full length gown of Blanc Neige. Approximately 6 × 20 g balls DMC Size 20 Cotton. Pair of 2.75 needles. Use ribbon through the holes at neck and lower yoke. Tie bows on each arm if desired.
Doll by Ria Warke.

Cast on 145 sts.
** Knit 3 rows.
Row 1: K1, *(m1, sl 1, k1, psso) twice, k3, (k2 tog, m1) twice, k1, repeat from * to end of row.
Row 2 and alternate rows: Purl.
Row 3: K1, *k1, (m1, sl 1, k1, psso) twice, k1, (k2 tog, m1) twice, k2, repeat from * to end of row.
Row 5: K3, *m1, sl 1, k1, psso, m1, sl 1, k2 tog, psso, m1, k2 tog, m1, k5, repeat from * to last 3 sts, k3.
Row 7: K1, *k1, (k2 tog, m1) twice, k1, (m1, sl 1, k1, psso) twice, k2, repeat from * to end of row.
Row 9: K1, *(k2 tog, m1) twice, k3, (m1, sl 1, k1, psso) twice, k1, repeat from * to end of row.
Row 11: (K2 tog, m1) twice, k5, *m1, sl 1, k1, psso, m1, sl 1, k2 tog, psso, m1, k2 tog, m1, k5, repeat from * to last 4 sts, (m1, sl 1, k1, psso) twice.
Row 12: Purl.
Repeat Rows 1–12 3 times.

Keeping continuity of pattern in panels, proceed as follows:
Row 1: K6, *pattern 13 sts, k11, repeat from * to last 6 sts, k6.
Row 2: Purl **.
Repeat Rows 1–2 until length required is reached (approx. 5'' or 12.5 cm for short version, 14'' or 36 cm for longer skirt). These measurements are approximate only; adjust the work to your size doll.

Keeping pattern panels work shaping:
Next Row: *** K6, (pattern 18 sts, k2 tog, pattern 22 sts, k2 tog, tbl, k4) twice, pattern 18 sts, k2 tog, pattern to end of row, work 9 rows.
Next Row: K6, (pattern 17 sts, k2 tog, pattern 21 sts, k2 tog, tbl, k4) twice, pattern 17 sts, k2 tog, pattern to end of row (135 sts), work 9 rows.
Next Row: K6, (pattern 17 sts, k2 tog, pattern 20 sts, k2 tog, tbl, k3) twice, pattern 17 sts, k2 tog, pattern to end of row *** (130 sts).
Continue until work measures approx. 11'' (28 cm) or 20'' (51 cm) for longer skirt, ending last row on *right* side.
Next Row: (K2 tog, k3 tog) 26 times (52 sts).
Leave sts on holder.

Right back

Cast on 73 sts.
Work as for front from ** – **.
Shaping ****.
Next Row: Pattern 24 sts, k2 tog, tbl, pattern 22 sts, k2 tog, pattern 19 sts, k2 tog, tbl, k2 (70 sts).
Work 9 rows.
Next Row: Pattern 23 sts, k2 tog, tbl, pattern 21 sts, k2 tog, pattern 18 sts, k2 tog, tbl, k2 (67 sts)

Work 9 rows.
Next Row: Pattern 23 sts, k2 tog, tbl, pattern 20 sts, k2 tog, pattern to end of row (65 sts)****.
Continue until work measures same as front to underarm, working last row on *right* side.
Next Row: K2 tog, (k2 tog, k3 tog) 12 times, k2 tog, k1, (27 sts).
Leave sts on holder.

Left back

Work to correspond with right back, working 1st shaping row thus:
K2, k2 tog, pattern 19 sts, k2 tog, tbl, pattern 22 sts, k2 tog, pattern to end.

Sleeves

Cast on 73 sts.
Knit 3 rows.
Work 5 rows in border pattern as for front of dress, knit one row.
Next Row: K1, *m1, k2 tog, k1, repeat from * to end of row.
Next Row: Knit.
Continue in border pattern, beginning with Row 7, until work measures approx. 4'' (10 cm) short version or 7½'' (19 cm) longer version, working last row on *right* side.
Next Row: (K2 tog) to last 3 sts, k3 tog, (36 sts).
Leave sts on holder.

Yoke

Right side of work facing, sl sts from st holders on to L.H. needles—27 sts from right back, 36 sts from 1st sleeve, 52 sts from front, 36 sts from 2nd sleeve, 27 sts from left back (178 sts).
Next Row: K3, *m1, k2 tog, k1, repeat from * to last st, k1.
Next Row: Knit.

Shaping

Row 1: K1, k2 tog, *k2, k2 tog, repeat from * to last 3 sts, k1, k2 tog (133 sts).
Row 2: Knit.
Row 3: K5, (k2 tog, k9) 11 times, k2 tog, knit to end of row (121 sts).
Knit 7 rows.
Row 11: K5, (k2 tog, k8) 11 times, k2 tog, knit to end of row (109 sts).

Knit 7 rows.

Row 19: K4, (k2 tog, k7) 11 times, k2 tog, knit to end of row (97 sts).

Knit 5 rows.

Row 25: K4, (k2 tog, k6) 11 times, k2 tog, knit to end of row (85 sts).

Knit 3 rows.

Row 29: K3, (k2 tog, k5) 11 times, k2 tog, knit to end of row (73 sts.)

Knit 3 rows.

Row 33: K3, (k2 tog, k4) 11 times, k2 tog, knit to end of row (61 sts).

Knit 2 rows.

Cast off.

Back band

Sew back seam to 1'' (2.5 cm) below beginning of yoke with right side facing, knit 28 sts down right side of back opening and 28 sts up left side of opening.

Next Row: Knit.

Row 2: K2, (m1, k2 tog, k5) 3 times, m1, k2 tog, knit to end of row.

Cast off.

Make up

Join side and sleeve seams to 2'' (5 cm) below beginning of yoke, join sleeve to front and back. Thread ribbon through wrist holes and below yoke. Secure ends of ribbons on wrong side. Sew on buttons. Press lightly if required.

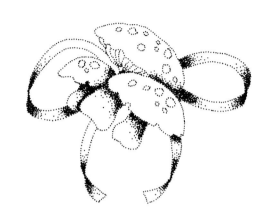

Dress: GOSSAMER

Reproduction Bru 22'' (56 cm).
A full length gown knitted in DMC Blanc 5200. Approximately 6 × 20 g balls Size 20 Cotton. Pair of
2.75 needles. Thread ribbon through holes at waist and wrists.
Doll courtesy Canberra Doll Club.

Cast on 159 sts.
Knit 2 rows.
Moss st 2 rows.
Row 1: K1, k2 tog, *k4, m1, k1, m1, k4, k3 tog, repeat from * to last 12 sts, k4, m1, k1, m1, k4, k2 tog, k1.
Row 2 and alternate rows: Purl.
Row 3: K1, k2 tog, *k3, (m1, k3) twice, k3 tog, repeat from * to last 12 sts, k3, (m1, k3) twice, k2 tog, k1.
Row 5: K1, k2 tog, *k2, m1, k1, m1, k3 tog, m1, k1, m1, k2, k3 tog, repeat from * to last 12 sts, k2, m1, k1, m1, k3 tog, m1, k1, m1, k2, k2 tog, k1.
Row 7: K1, k2 tog, *k1, m1, k3, m1, k2 tog, k2, m1, k1, k3 tog, repeat from * until last 12 sts, k1, m1, k3, m1, k2 tog, k2, m1, k1, k2 tog, k1.
Row 9: K1, k2 tog, *m1, k1, m1, k3 tog, repeat from * to last 4 sts, m1, k1, m1, k2 tog, k1.
Row 10: Purl.
Repeat Rows 1–10 12 times (adjust length of skirt to your requirements).
Decrease for waist:
Row 1: K1, (k2 tog) 38 times, k4, (k2 tog) 39 times.
Row 2: Moss st 39, p4, moss st 39.
Row 3: Moss st 39, k4, moss st 39.
Row 4: Moss st 39, p4, moss st 39.
Work row of ribbon holes *k1, m1, k2 tog, repeat from * to end of row. Purl back.
Proceed as follows, right side facing:
Row 1: Moss st 39, k2 tog, m1, k2 tog, moss st 39.
Row 2: Moss st 39, p1, (k1, p1) in m1 of previous row, p1, moss st 39.
Row 3: Cast off 2 sts, moss st 37, k4, moss st 39.
Row 4: Cast off 2 sts, moss st 37, p4, moss st 37.
Row 5: K2 tog, moss st 33, (k2 tog, m1, k2 tog) twice, moss st 33, k2 tog.
Row 6: K2 tog, moss st 32, (p1, k1, p1 in m1 of previous row, p1) twice, moss st 32, k2 tog.
Row 7: K2 tog, moss st 31, k8, moss st 31, k2 tog.
Row 8: K2 tog, moss st 30, p8, moss st 30, k2 tog.
Row 9: Moss st 29, (k2 tog, m1, k2 tog) 3 times, moss st 29.
Row 10: Moss st 29, (p1, k1, p1 in m1 of previous row, p1) 3 times, moss st 29.
Row 11: Moss st 29, k12, moss st 29.
Row 12: Moss st 29, p12, moss st 29.
Row 13: Moss st 27, (k2 tog, m1, k2 tog) 4 times, moss st 27.
Row 14: Moss st 27, (p1, k1, p1 in m1 of previous row, p1) 4 times, moss st 27.
Row 15: Moss st 27, k16, moss st 27.
Row 16: Moss st 27, p16, moss st 27.
Continue in this way, having 4 extra pattern sts in centre, and 2 less moss sts each side, on the next row and every following 4th row until you have 36 pattern sts in centre, and 17 moss sts each side. Proceed as follows:

Row 1: Moss st 15, k2 tog, m1, k2 tog, k2, moss st 28, k2, k2 tog, m1, k2 tog, moss st 15.
Row 2: Moss st 15, p1, k1, p1 in m1 of previous row, p1, k2, moss st 28, k2, p1, k1, p1 in m1 of previous row, p1, moss st 15.
Row 3: Moss st 15, k6, place these 21 sts on st holder, cast off 28 sts for neck, k6, moss st 15.
Work on the last 21 sts for shoulder, and right half of back.
Row 1: Moss st 15, p4, k2.
Row 2: K2, k2 tog, m1, k2 tog, moss st 15.
Row 3: Moss st 15, p1, k1, p1 in m1 of previous row, p1, k2.
Row 4: K6, moss st 15.
Repeat Rows 1–4 once.
Row 9: Moss st 15, p4, k2, cast on 17 sts.
Row 10: K into back of 17 sts, cast on, k2, k2 tog, m1, k2 tog, moss st 15.
Row 11: Moss st 15, p1, k1, p1 in m1 of previous row, p1, moss st 15, k2 tog, m1, k2.
Row 12: K2, moss st 17, k4, moss st 15.
Row 13: Moss st 15, p4, moss st 17, k2
Row 14: K1, (k2 tog, m1, k2 tog) 5 times, moss st 17.
Row 15: Moss st 17, (p1, k1, p1 in m1 of previous row, p1) 5 times, k1.
Row 16: K21, moss st 17.
Row 17: **Work in moss st, ending row k2.
Row 18: K2, work in moss st to end of row.
Row 19: Work in moss st until last 4 sts, k2 tog, m1, k2.
Row 20: As Row 18.
Row 21: As Row 17.
Row 22: As Row 18.
Row 23: As Row 17.
Row 24: As Row 18.
Repeat from ** until back measures same as front to armhole shaping. Cast on 2 sts at armhole edge of next row and following 2 alternate rows. Work 4 rows moss st. Cast off.
Return to sts on st holder. Join yarn at neck edge.
Row 1: K2, p4, moss st 15.
Row 2: Moss st 15, k2 tog, m1, k2 tog, k2.
Row 3: K2, p1, k1, p1 in m1 of previous row, p1, moss st 15.
Row 4: Moss st 15, k6.
Repeat Rows 1–3 once.
Row 9: As Row 1.
Row 10: Moss st 15, k2 tog, m1, k2 tog, k2, cast on 17 sts.
Row 11: K into back of 17 sts cast on. K2, p1, k1, p1 in m1 of previous row, p1, moss st 15.
Row 12: Moss st 15, k4, moss st 17, k2.
Row 13: K2, moss st 17, p4, moss st 15.
Row 14: Moss st 17, (k2 tog, m1, k2 tog) 5 times, k1.
Row 15: K1, (p1, k1, p1 in m1 of previous row, p1) 5 times, moss st 17.

Row 16: Moss st 17, k21.
Row 17: K2, moss st to end of row.
Continue in moss st to correspond with right back, omitting buttonholes.
Knit the back of skirt the same as front until after the decreasing for waist. Cast off. Place the buttonhole edge of back yoke over the left half for approx. 1.5 cm (½''). Sew into position. Then sew on back skirt.

Sleeves

Cast on 75 sts.
Knit 2 rows.
Work in dress pattern for 6 rows. Proceed as follows:
Row 1: *K1, k2 tog, repeat from * to end of row.
Row 2: Purl.
Row 3: K2, *m1, k2 tog, repeat from * to end of row.
Row 4: Purl.
Row 5: K6, knit in f & b of every st until 7 sts remain, k7 (87 sts).
Row 6: Purl.
Work in pattern for 14 rows. Shape top thus:
Row 1: Cast off 3 sts, k3, (includes st left on needle from cast off). M1, k3 tog, m1, k1, m1, k2, k3 tog, work as Row 5 of pattern from * to end of row.
Row 2: Cast off 3 sts, purl to end of row.
Row 3: Cast off 3 sts, m1, k2 tog, k2, m1, k1, k3 tog, work as Row 7 of pattern from * until 9 sts remain, k1, m1, k3, m1, k2 tog, k3.
Row 4: As Row 2.
Row 5: Cast off 3 sts, k3, (including st already on needle), m1, k3 tog, work as Row 9 of pattern from * until 6 sts remain, m1, k1, m1, k3 tog, m1, k2.
Row 6: As Row 2.
Row 7: Cast off 3 sts, k2 tog, work same as Row 3 of pattern to last 6 sts, k2 tog, k4.
Row 8: As Row 2.
Row 9: Cast off 3 sts, k2 tog, (m1, k3) twice, k3 tog, work as Row 3 of sleeve from * to end of row.
Row 10: Cast off 3 sts, p10, (including st already on needle), p2 tog until 9 sts remain, p9.
Cast off.

Frill for yoke

Cast on 99 sts.
Work 1st six rows of skirt pattern. Cast off.

Make up

Press work. Sew side and sleeve seams. Insert sleeves, placing seam to under arm. Sew frill around lace on yoke. Sew on buttons to correspond with buttonholes. Work picot edging around neck. Thread ribbon through sleeves. Trim front of yoke with ribbon bow, with long ends if desired.

Bonnet

Cast on 13 sts.
Work 5 rows moss st.
Next Row: K1, *m1, k1, repeat from * to end of row.
Work 5 rows moss st.
Repeat last 6 rows twice (97 sts).
Next Row: Knit, inc 4 times at intervals in row (101 sts).
Next Row: Purl.

Pattern
Row 1: K2, k2 tog, *k4, m1, k1, m1, k4, k3 tog, repeat from * until last 13 sts, k4, m1, k1, m1, k4, k2 tog, k2.
Row 2 and alternate rows: K2, purl to last 2 sts, k2.
Row 3: K2, k2 tog, *k3, (m1, k3) twice, k3 tog, repeat from * until last 13 sts, k3 (m1, k3) twice, k2 tog, k2.
Row 5: K2, k2 tog, *k2, m1, k1, m1, k3 tog, m1, k1, m1, k2, k3 tog, repeat from * until last 13 sts, k2, m1, k1, m1, k3 tog, m1, k1, m1, k2, k2 tog, k2.
Row 7: K2, k2 tog, *k1, m1, k3, m1, k2 tog, k2, m1, k1, k3 tog, repeat from * until last 13 sts, k1, m1, k3, m1, k2 tog, k2, m1, k1, k2 tog, k2.
Row 9: K2, k2 tog, *m1, k1, m1, k3 tog, repeat from * until last 5 sts, m1, k1, m1, k2 tog, k2.
Row 10: As Row 2.
Repeat Pattern Rows 1–10 5 times. Cast off.

Frill for bonnet

Cast on 99 sts.
Knit 2 rows.
Work in skirt pattern for 7 rows.
Row 8: *P3 tog, p9, repeat from * to last 3 sts, p3 tog.
Work 3 rows moss st.
Cast off.
Sew frill to cast-off edge of bonnet. Sew back of bonnet for approx. 2¾'' (7 cm). Attach ribbon ties at front of bonnet to tie under chin.

Dress: ROSIE

Antique Simon & Halbig 22'' (56 cm).
A mid calf length dress in DMC Blanc 5200 Size 20. Approximately 6 × 20 g balls. Pair 2.75 needles.
Ribbon ties at neck, waist, sleeves. Ribbons tied in bows close back of dress. Neck brooch made from a
knitted flower. The doll wears a bobble bonnet knitted in 3-ply cotton using 1 × 50 g ball. Pair of 2.75
needles. Wide ribbon bow at back of bonnet. There is a slight variation in the patterns. The doll on page 25
wears the original design.
Doll from the author's collection.

Cast on 229 sts.
Row 1: Knit.
Row 2: Purl.
Row 3: Knit.
Row 4: K1, *m1, k4, sl 1, k2 tog, psso, k4, m1, k1, repeat from * to end of row.
Row 5: Purl.
Row 6: As Row 4.
Row 7: Knit.
Row 8: Purl.
Row 9: Knit.
Row 10: As Row 4.
Row 11: Purl.
Row 12: As Row 4.
Row 13: Knit.
Row 14: Purl.
Row 15: Knit.
Row 16: Knit.
Row 17: (K1, p1) to end of row.
Repeat Row 17 10 times.
Row 28: Knit.
Row 29: Knit.
Row 30: Purl.
Row 31: Knit.
Row 32: As Row 4.
Row 33: Purl.
Row 34: As Row 4.
Row 35: Knit.
Row 36: Purl.
Row 37: Knit.
Row 38: As Row 4.
Row 39: Purl.
Row 40: As Row 4.
Row 41: Knit.
Row 42: Purl.
Row 43: Knit.
Row 44: As Row 4.
Row 45: Purl.
Row 46: As Row 4.
Row 47: Knit.
Row 48: Purl.
Row 49: Knit.
Row 50: Knit.
Row 51: (K1, p1) to end of row.
Repeat Row 51 10 times.
Knit 2 rows, purl one row, knit 2 rows, decreasing 3 sts along last row (226 sts).
Begin ribbed pattern of skirt.
Row 1: Sl 1, k2, p4, k1, p2, *k2, p4, k1, p2, repeat from * to end of row.
Row 2: Sl 1, p1, k1, p1, k3, p2, k1, *p1, k1, p1, k3, p2, k1, repeat from * to end of row.
Row 3: Sl 1, p2, *k2, p2, k1, p4, repeat from * to last 2 sts, p2.
Row 4: Sl 1, (p1, k1) twice, p2, k3, *(p1, k1) twice, p2,

k3, repeat from * to end of row.
Repeat Rows 1–4 6 times or until length desired is reached.
Purl 1 row.

Waistband

Row 1: K2 tog to end of row (114 sts).
Row 2: Knit.
Row 3: Purl.
Row 4: Knit.
Row 5: Knit.
Row 6: (K1, p1) to end of row.
Row 7: K1, (m1, k2 tog) to end of row.
Row 8: (K1, p1) to end of row.
Row 9: Knit.
Row 10: Knit.
Row 11: Purl.
Row 12: Knit.
Row 13: Knit.

Bodice

Repeat ribbed pattern of skirt (the rows end with same patterned rib as they begin). Repeat the 4 rows 6 times.

Left back

Knit 32 sts in pattern, turn, work for 29 rows. On armhole side knit 8 rows of 9 sts for shoulder. Cast off these 9 sts, leaving 23 sts on needle.

Front

Knit 50 sts in pattern, turn, work for 28 rows, then knit 8 rows on 9 sts. Cast off these 9 sts, knit again across front, work the last 9 sts in same manner, cast off these 9 sts, retaining 32 middle sts on needle.

Right back

Knit remaining 32 sts for 28 rows. Knit 8 rows on 9 sts, cast off these 9 sts, sew shoulder pieces together.

Neck

Row 1: With right side of work towards you, knit across left back, pick up and knit 14 sts across shoulder. Knit across front, pick up and knit 14 sts on the other

shoulder, knit across right back.
Row 2: Knit.
Row 3: Purl.
Row 4: Knit.
Row 5: Knit.
Row 6: K1, m1, k2 tog, repeat to end of row.
Row 7: Knit.
Row 8: Knit.
Row 9: Purl.
Cast off.

Sleeve

Cast on 46 sts.
Work 14 rows, k1, p1, rib.
Row 15: Knit.
Row 16: Knit.
Row 17: Purl.
Row 18: Knit.
Row 19: Knit.
Row 20: K1, *m1, k2 tog, repeat from * to end of row.
Row 21: Knit.
Row 22: Knit.
Row 23: Purl.
Row 24: Work in ribbed pattern of the skirt. Knit 4 rows, inc 1 st at end of every 4th row until you have 52 sts. Work 14 repeats of ribbed pattern. Cast off. Work the other sleeve in same way but inc. at beginning of the rows. The increased side is the underside of sleeve. Sew neatly into armholes, work 1dc, 5ch. Miss 2 sts of knitting and repeat around neck and sleeves. Thread ribbon through neck, waist and wrists. The ribbons are tied in bows down the back of the garment and the back seam of dress remains open.

Bobble bonnet

Cast on 86 sts.
Knit 4 rows in k2, p2, rib.
Row 5: Knit.
Row 6: Purl.
Row 7: Knit.
Row 8: Purl.
Row 9: Knit.
Row 10: Purl.
Knit 4 rows.
Row 15: Purl.
Row 16: Knit.
Row 17: Purl.
In the next row the bobbles begin. Make bobbles thus: Cast on 3 sts, k next st off L.H. needle. Turn, sl 1st st purlwise. Knit 3 sts, turn, p3 sts, turn, k3 sts, turn, p3 tog, draw next st over 3p tog sts. Work thus when

pattern reads mb.
Row 18: K5, *mb, k4, repeat from * to end of row.
Row 19: Purl.
Row 20: Knit.
Row 21: Purl.
Row 22: Knit 3 rows.
Repeat from Row 15.
Row 35: Purl.
Row 36: Knit.
Repeat Rows 35 and 36 3 times.
Row 43: Knit.
Row 44: Knit.
Row 45: Commence crown of bonnet. P57, turn, leaving 29 sts on L.H. needle, k3, *mb, k4, repeat from * 5 times, k2 tog, tbl, turn, p27, p2 tog, turn, k27, k2 tog, turn, p27, p2 tog. Continue working in this manner, mbs in every 6th row, knitting between purled rows, decreasing 1 st at the end of every row, until only 27 sts remain. Cast off the 27 crown sts.
For back frill, cast on 146 sts, work st st for 46 rows, rib 4 rows (k2, p2). Cast off.
Sew the back frill to bonnet by the cast-off sts.

Front frilling

Cast on 86 sts.
Row 1: Knit.
Row 2: M1, k1, repeat to end of row.
Row 3: Knit.
Row 4: M1, k1, repeat to end of row.
Row 5: Knit.
Row 6: Knit.
Cast off loosely.
Sew this frilling around front of bonnet, attaching the cast on sts to the row next to the 1st 4 ribbed rows. The frill will fall into an even fullness if correctly sewn.

Knit 2nd frill

Cast on 86 sts.
Repeat Rows 1–4.
Cast off on completion of 5th row. Sew this frill to the middle of the 9 knit rows before commencement of crown.

Frill to edge back frill

Cast on 146 sts. Knit as 2nd frill. Sew it to last k row before ribbing. Make a cord; run it through where back frill joins bonnet. Have cord long enough to tie under chin. Decorate with ribbons if desired.

Reproduction Kestner 18'' (46 cm).
The dress was knitted on 2 mm (14) needles using 6 balls of DMC Blanc 5200, Size 20 Cotton. Ribbon
ties at waist, sleeves and wide neck. The dress, which opens down the back, is fastened with ribbon bows.
These two photographs show how you can vary the style of a gown, by length, size of needle, or change of
ribbing.
Doll by Pat Blyth.

Dress: LUCY

Antique Simon & Halbig 13'' (33 cm).
This little dress dates from the 1860s. Use 2.75 needles and 2 × 20 g balls DMC Size 20 Cotton. You should have ample thread for the hat as well. The hat is from the pattern Demelza, knitted on size 2.75 needles also.
Doll from the author's collection.

Cast on 12 sts for pleated edging.
Row 1: Knit.
Row 2: Purl.
Row 3: Knit.
Row 4: Purl.
Row 5: Purl.
Row 6: Knit.
Row 7: Purl.
Row 8: Knit.
Sl the 1st st of every row. Repeat Rows 1–8 24 times. Cast off on Row 8, leaving last st on needle. Pick up and knit 100 sts across pleated edge and commence skirt pattern thus:
Row 1: Purl.
Row 2: Knit.
Row 3: Purl.
Row 4: Knit.
Row 5: Purl.
Row 6: With wrong side of work facing, *(k1, p1) twice in 1st st, p4 tog, repeat from * to end of row.
Row 7: Purl (100 sts).
Row 8: Knit.
Row 9: Purl.
Row 10: Knit.
Row 11: Purl.
Row 12: With wrong side of work facing, *p4 tog, (k1, p1) twice in next st, repeat from * to end of row.
Repeat Rows 1–12.
Row 25: K2, p2 to end of row.
Repeat Row 25 9 times.
Row 35: (K2, p2) 4 times, (p2 tog, k2) 3 times, p2 tog, (k2, p2) 8 times, (p2 tog, k2) 3 times, p2 tog, (k2, p2) 5 times (92 sts).
Row 36: Work in k2, p2, rib, knitting 1 st where decreases occurred.
Row 37: (K2, p2) 4 times, (k2, p2 tog) 4 times, (k2, p2) 8 times, (k2, p2 tog) 4 times, (k2, p2) 5 times (84 sts). Work 7 rows in k2, p2, rib.

1st half of back

(K1, p1) 10 times, turn, rib back.
Repeat 8 times. Cast off.
Resume work where you divided. Cast off 2 sts for armhole, k1, p1, rib for 38 sts, turn, rib back. Repeat 8 times, cast off centre 30 sts on each side, rib 4 sts for 16 rows. Cast off. Resume work where divided. Cast off 2 sts, (k1, p1) to end of row (22 sts). Turn, rib back, repeat 8 times. Cast off. Sew shoulder pieces in position on the back pieces of dress.

Sleeves

Cast on 30 sts, knit 18 rows.
Row 19: K3, (k2 tog) 12 times, k3 (18 sts).
Work in k1, p1, rib for 8 rows or length desired. Cast off. Make another sleeve. Sew into armholes, sew up back of dress to k1, p1, rib.
Work neck edging thus: 1 dc in each st, *3 ch, miss 2 sts, 1 dc in next st, repeat from *, fasten off.
Press the dress. Thread narrow ribbon through neck edge.

Cape

Cast on 40 sts.
K1, p1, rib for 8 rows.
Row 9: Sl 1, (k1, p1, k1) in next st, *k1, (k1, p1, k1) in next st, repeat from * to end of row.
Row 10: Purl (80 sts).
Row 11: *(K1, p1, k1) in 1st st, p3 tog, repeat from * to end of row.
Row 12: Purl.
Row 13: *P3 tog, (k1, p1, k1) in next st, repeat from * to end of row.
Row 14: Purl.
Repeat from Row 11 twice. Cast off loosely.
Finish cape with crochet edge at bottom R.H. side, 1 sc *3 ch, miss 1 or 2 sts of knitting, 1 dc. Repeat from *. Continue around cape. Thread narrow ribbon through neck edge.

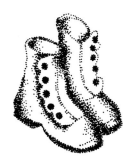

Tucked Dress: CLEMENTINE

A wooden doll 20'' (51 cm) high carved from Tasmanian celerytop pine, with a wig made from Lincoln wool and body of cloth.

Clementine is wearing a simple tucked gown knitted in DMC 5200 Cotton, size 20, using 2 mm (14) needles. You will need 6 × 20 g balls of cotton, six buttons, and a small length of ribbon to tie at waist. Doll carved by Jan Clements of Yackandandah. From the author's collection.

Front

Cast on 105 sts.
**Work 12 rows st st. (Begin the work with a knit row.)
Row 13: Purl. This row makes hemline ridge.
Work 13 rows st st, beginning with a purl row.
Make the hem by knitting 1 st from the needle tog with 1 st from cast on edge, continue thus until end of row.
Work 25 rows in st st.
Next Row: Purl.
Work 9 rows st st, beginning with a purl row.
Make tuck by folding work on purl ridge, counting down 9 rows from purl ridge on wrong side of work and knitting 1 st from needle tog with 1 st from 10th row. Continue thus to end of row.
Work 23 rows in st st, beginning with a purl row.
Next Row: Purl.
Work 7 rows st st, beginning with a purl row.
Make second tuck thus: Fold work on purl ridge as before and knit 1 st from needle tog with 1 st from 8th row, continue thus to end of row.
Work 21 rows in st st, beginning with a purl row.
Next Row: Purl.
Work 5 rows st st, beginning with a purl row.
Make third tuck thus: Knit 1 st from needle tog with 1 st from 6th row, continue thus to end of row.
Work 19 rows st st, beginning with a purl row.
Next Row: Purl.
Work 3 rows in st st, beginning with a purl row.
Make fourth tuck thus: Knit 1 st from needle tog with 1 st from 4th row, continue thus to end of row.
Continue in st st, beginning with a purl row.
*Adjust length of skirt to your requirements, ending with knit row.***

Skirt shaping:
P1, *p2 tog, repeat from * to end of row (53 sts).
Work 14 rows in st st.

Row of ribbon holes worked thus:
K4, m1, *k5, m1, repeat from * to last 4 sts, k4 (63 sts).
Continue in st st for approximately 5'' (12 cm).

Armhole shaping:
Cast off 4 sts at beg of next 2 rows.
Dec 1 st at each end of every row until 49 sts remain.

Neck shaping:
Next Row: K12, turn, leave remaining sts on spare needle.
Work 17 rows st st on the 12 sts. Cast off.
Slip centre 25 sts onto spare needle. Rejoin cotton, knit to end. Complete to correspond with 1st side.

Back

Work as front from **–**.

Shape skirt:
P1, (p2 tog) 26 times. Turn, leave remaining sts on spare needle. Continue on these 27 sts for 1st side as follows:
Cast on 2 sts, k to end (29 sts).
K5 sts at centre back edge on every row. Work 13 rows in st st.

Row of ribbon holes worked thus:
K7, m1, *k5, m1. Repeat from * to last 2 sts, k2 (34 sts).
Continue in st st until back measures the same as front to armhole, ending with a knit row.

Shape armhole:
Cast off 4 sts at beg of next row.
Dec 1 st at armhole edge in every row until 27 sts remain.
Work until neck shaping, ending with wrong side row.

Shape neck:
Slip 1st 15 sts onto stitch holder. Join cotton to remaining 12 sts. Work in st st until back matches front armhole edge. Cast off.
With wrong side facing join cotton to remaining 52 sts. Cast on 3 sts, k3, (k2 tog) twice, (p2 tog) 24 times (29 sts). Work in st st to match the other side, reversing all shapings, and making 6 buttonholes, evenly spaced.

The buttonhole row:
With right side facing knit to last 4 sts, k2 tog, m1, k2.

Sleeves

Make 2.
Cast on 38 sts.
Work 4 rows in st st, beginning with a knit row.
Next Row: Purl.
Work 5 rows in st st, beginning with a purl row.
Make the hem in sleeve as for skirt.
Next Row: P1, *m1, p1, repeat from * to end of row (75 sts).
Continue in st st until length desired, approximately 5'' (12 cm).
End with purl row.

Sleeve shaping:
Cast off 4 sts at beginning of the next two rows.
Dec 1 st both ends of every row until 39 sts remain.
K1, *k2 tog, repeat from * to end of row (20 sts). Cast off.
Sew shoulder seams, and work neck thus: With right side facing begin at left side of back opening, knit 15 sts from holder, pick up, and knit 8 sts up left side of back, 16 sts down left side of front, knit 25 sts from centre. Pick

up and knit 16 sts up right side of front, 8 sts down right side of back, then knit 15 sts from the holder (103 sts).

Rows 1, 3 and 5: K5, p to last 5 sts, k5.

Row 2: K13, k2 tog, tbl, k2 tog, k20, k2 tog, tbl, k2 tog, k21, k2 tog, tbl, k2 tog, k20, k2 tog, tbl, k2 tog, k13 (95 sts).

Row 4: K12, k2 tog, tbl, k2 tog, k18, k2 tog, tbl, k2 tog, k19, k2 tog, tbl, k2 tog, k18, k2 tog, tbl, k2 tog, k8, k2 tog, m1, k2 (87 sts).

Row 6: K11, k2 tog, tbl, k2 tog, k16, k2 tog, tbl, k2 tog, k17, k2 tog, tbl, k2 tog, k16, k2 tog, tbl, k2 tog, k11 (79 sts).

Next Row: Cast off 5 sts, knit to end of row.

Next Row: Cast off 5 sts, k6, inc in next 2 sts, k16, inc in next 2 sts, k17, inc in next 2 sts, k16, inc in next 2 sts, k6 (77 sts).

Purl next row.

Next Row: K7, inc in next 2 sts, k18, inc in next 2 sts, k19, inc in next 2 sts, k18, inc in next 2 sts, k7 (85 sts).

Purl next row.

Next Row: K8, inc in next 2 sts, k20, inc in next 2 sts, k21, inc in next 2 sts, k20, inc in next 2 sts, k8 (93 sts). Cast off purlwise.

Press work lightly, and assemble thus: Sew up side and sleeve seams. Set in sleeves, adjusting fullness. Fold neck border in half, sl st into position. Press tucks to form firm edges. Sew on buttons.

Dress: MARTHA

Reproduction 'Miranda' doll 18'' (46 cm).
Dressed in khaki silk—approximately 100 g 3-ply silk knitted on 2 mm (14) needles. The dress is worn
over a finely striped frock, the sleeves and neckline buttonholed in the silk of the dress. The tiny cuffs have
bullion stitch buttons. Nora wears another version of the knitted dress on page 32.
Doll by Aileen Sellen.

Skirt

Cast on 200 sts. Knit 1 row.
Row 1: Sl 1, *m1, k2 tog, k2, repeat from * to end of row.
Row 2: Sl 1, k1, *m1, k2 tog, k2, repeat from *, ending row k1.
Repeat Rows 1–2 30 times.
Work approx. 5'' (13 cm) in garter st, adjusting length as desired.
Work 6 rows st st, then a row of holes thus: k2, (m1, k2 tog), k1 to end of row.
Work 6 rows st st.

Bodice

Row 1: Sl 1, k2, *k2 tog, k2, repeat from * to last 3 sts, k3.
Row 2: Sl 1, purlwise, p1, *p2 tog, p1, repeat from * to last 3 sts, k3 (102 sts).
Knit 20 rows.
Divide and work sts as follows:
Row 1: Knit 38 rows on 1st 28 sts. Leave on holder.
Row 2: Knit 21 rows on 46 sts. Leave on holder.
Row 3: Knit 38 rows on 28 sts.
Row 4: Knit across all sts. Cast off loosely.

Sleeves

Cast on 36 sts.
Work 28 rows in skirt pattern. Cast off. Press lightly.
Sew back of skirt to waistband. Sew in sleeves, sew sleeve seam.
Crochet around skirt, sleeves and neck as follows: *3tr, 1ch, 1dc, 1ch, repeat from *.
Sew 5 buttons down back using holes in crochet as buttonholes. Thread ribbon through waistband, tie at back. If preferred, use ribbon ties down back of the dress instead of buttons.

Dress: NORA

Antique A.M. 370 16'' (40 cm).
This beautiful doll is wearing another version of Martha (page 31). The skirt has been lengthened to reach the ankles. A wide ribbon sash ties at the back. Her bonnet and shoulder covering are made from the Bobble Bonnet pattern. (For instructions see Rosie, page 22.) Nora has the curtain of her bonnet brought around the shoulders, while Rosie has hers tied back with a wide bow. This is a versatile design. You will need 5 × 20 g DMC Blanc 5200 Size 20 and 2 mm (14) needles. Bobble bonnet requires 50 g 3-ply cotton, 2.75 (12) needles.
Doll courtesy of James Botham.

Skirt

Cast on 200 sts. Knit 1 row.
Row 1: Sl 1, *m1, k2 tog, k2, repeat from * to end of row.
Row 2: Sl 1, k1, *m1, k2 tog, k2, repeat from *, ending row k1.
Repeat Rows 1–2 30 times.
Work at least 5'' (13 cm) in garter stitch, adjusting length as needed so that the finished skirt will reach to the doll's ankles.
Work 6 rows st st, then a row of holes thus: k2, (m1, k2 tog), k1 to end of row.
Work 6 rows st st.

Bodice

Row 1: Sl 1, k2, *k2 tog, k2, repeat from * to last 3 sts, k3.
Row 2: Sl 1, purlwise, p1, *p2 tog, p1, repeat from * to last 3 sts, k3 (102 sts).

Knit 20 rows.
Divide and work sts as follows:
Row 1: Knit 38 rows on 1st 28 sts. Leave on holder.
Row 2: Knit 21 rows on 46 sts. Leave on holder.
Row 3: Knit 38 rows on 28 sts.
Row 4: Knit across all sts. Cast off loosely.

Sleeves

Cast on 36 sts.
Work 28 rows in skirt pattern. Cast off. Press lightly.
Sew back of skirt to waistband. Sew in sleeves, sew sleeve seam.
Crochet around skirt, sleeves and neck as follows: *3tr, 1ch, 1dc, 1ch, repeat from *.
Sew 5 buttons down back using holes in crochet as buttonholes. Thread ribbon through waistband, tie at back. If preferred, use ribbon ties down back of the dress instead of buttons.

Nora is standing beside the Botham bed, a superb nineteenth century brass domed bed of exceptional craftsmanship which still has its original damask hangings. All the bedding is trimmed with knitted lace. The bed-chest, a little piece of English oak, is about eighty years old. Bed dimensions: height 2'8'' (77 cm), width 12'' (30 cm), length 1'9'' (50 cm).

Cosy Coat and Cap: HOLLY

This outfit is suitable for a doll with a toddler body, approximately size 24'' (61 cm).
Knitted in 4-ply cotton on 2.75 (12) needles. You will need 4 × 50 g balls and 6 buttons. The length of the coat can be adjusted to suit the doll.

Cast on 77 sts.
Knit 12 rows.

Back

Row 1: *K2, p3, repeat from * ending row with k2.
Row 2: Purl.
Row 3: Knit.
Row 4: P2, *k3, p2, repeat from * to end of row.
Repeat from Row 1 until 88 rows of pattern have been worked. Decrease at both ends of 12th row, and every 12th row, until 5 sts have been decreased at both ends of needle. Keep pattern correct while decreasing. The distinct rib formed by pattern will assist in keeping pattern correct. Armhole is reached after 88th row. Should you desire a longer garment work extra rows before shaping armholes.
Shape armholes thus:
Row 1: Cast off 2 sts, work in pattern to end of row.
Row 2: Cast off 2 sts, work in pattern to end of row.
Row 3: Decrease 1 st at beginning of next 10 rows (53 sts).
Work 12 rows on the 53 sts without shaping. Then cast off 2 sts at beginning of every row until 17 sts remain. Cast off.

Right front

Cast on 54 sts.
Knit 12 rows.
Row 1: K6 (these are border sts), p3, *k2, p3, repeat from * to end of row.
Row 2: Purl to last 6 sts, k6.
Row 3: Knit.
Row 4: *K3, p2, repeat to last 9 sts, k9.
Continue working as above, decreasing 1 st at underarm end of every 12th row until 5 sts have been decreased. Continue in pattern without further shaping until 89 rows have been worked.
Shape armholes thus:
Row 90: Cast off 2 sts, work to end of row.
Row 91: Work in pattern.
Repeat last 2 rows until 10 sts have been decreased. Work 23 rows in pattern without shaping. Cast off 9 sts at front edge of coat, work in pattern to end of row. Cast off 2 sts, work in pattern to end of row. Repeat last row until 1 st remains. Cast off.

Left front

Shape as for right front, but front border will be at *end* of 1st pattern row of left front, underarm decreasings

will be at *opposite end* of needle.
Knit 12 rows.
Row 1: P3, *k2, p3, repeat from * to end of row, k6 for front border.
Row 2: K6, purl to end of row.
Row 3: Knit.
Row 4: K6, *k3, p2, repeat from * to end of row, ending k3.
Continue as right front, doing exactly the same shaping at side, underarm, and neck. Cast off.

Sleeves

Work 2 as follows:
Cast on 30 sts.
Knit 20 rows.
Row 1: *K2, p3, repeat from * to end of row.
Row 2: Purl.
Row 3: Knit.
Row 4: *K3, p2, repeat from * to end of row.
Repeat these 4 rows.
Work inc as follows:
Pick up loop under 2nd st, knitting or purling according to pattern. Continue to last 2 sts.
Increase in same manner, keeping pattern correct, every 5th row, until 7 increases have been worked (47 sts).
Work 6 rows in pattern.
Cast off 2 sts at beginning of each row until 16 sts remain. Cast off.

Collar

Cast on 3 sts.
Inc each end of needle until you have 15 sts. Knit until length required.
K2 tog each end of needle until 3 sts remain.
Cast off.
Sew collar to coat, adjusting fullness. Neck of coat can be finished with crochet if preferred.

Press the coat pieces lightly, taking care not to flatten rib pattern. Sew up seams. Work loop buttonholes to the size of your buttons. Turn back cuffs on sleeves.

Cap

Cast on 112 sts.
Work 40 rows in garter st.
Repeat coat pattern 6 times. Cast off.
Fold so that garter st forms band of hat. Sew across top and down side of hat. Fold corners onto brim, sew button on each corner, taking thread through crown and brim.

Baby Doll Ensemble: DEMELZA

Under petticoat

Cast on 100 sts.
Knit until work measures 8'' (20 cm).
Row 1: K2 tog until end of row (50 sts).
Row 2: Knit.
Row 3: K2, *m1, k2 tog, repeat from * to end of row.
Continue in garter st for 3'' (7.5 cm), then make a row of holes as Row 3.
Knit the next row. Cast off.

The petticoat is open in front. Thread ribbon or fine chain cord through holes. The top ribbon or cord ties around doll's body under the arms, and the other around the waist. The skirt is folded over doll's legs.

Top petticoat

Using 4 needles cast on 80 sts (28 sts on each of 2 needles, 24 sts on 3rd needle).
Round 1: Knit.
Round 2: *M1, k2 tog, repeat from * to end of round.
Round 3: Knit.
Round 4: K19, draw the last st but one over last st, k1, draw another st over, repeat until 6 sts are cast off for armhole, k35, work another armhole, k16.
Round 5: K17, cast on 6 sts, k34, cast on 6 sts, k17, continue in k2, p2, ribbing for 4'' (10 cm).
Next Round: *M1, k1, repeat from * to end of round (160 sts).
Round 1: *K4, p4, repeat from * to end of round.
Work 3 rounds of skirt in k4, p4, rib.
Round 5: *P4, k4, repeat from * to end of round.
Work 3 rounds in p4, k4, rib.
Repeat from Round 1 of skirt until work measures 9'' (23 cm).
Cast off loosely.

Lace border

Cast on 11 sts.
Row 1: Sl 1, k2 tog, m1, k1, (m1, k2 tog) 3 times, m1, k1.
Row 2 and every alternate row: Knit.
Row 3: Sl 1, k2 tog, m1, k2, (m1, k2 tog) 3 times, m1, k1.
Row 5: Sl 1, k2 tog, m1, k3, (m1, k2 tog) 3 times, m1, k1.
Row 7: Sl 1, k2 tog, m1, k4, (m1, k2 tog) 3 times, m1, k1.
Row 9: Sl 1, k2 tog, m1, k5, (m1, k2 tog) 3 times, m1, k1.
Row 11: Sl 1, k2 tog, m1, k6, (m1, k2 tog) 3 times, m1, k1.
Row 12: Cast off 6 sts. K10.
Repeat Rows 1–12 until length required to edge petticoat. Press the edging and sew neatly onto petticoat. Strengthen armholes with double crochet. Make chain, or use ribbon, to thread through holes. Tie in bows at back of petticoat.

Half petticoat

Cast on 160 sts.
Work pattern for top petticoat from Round 1 of skirt until work measures 9'' (23 cm). Knit 2 rows. Ribbon holes in next row, k2, m1, k2 tog, knit 2 rows. Cast off loosely. Sew up back seam. Knit lace border to length required to edge petticoat.

Robe

Cast on 50 sts.
Front: Knit 5 rows.

From the original pattern published in the nineteenth century: 'The doll represented in the accompanying engraving will gladden the hearts of little people, and afford endless amusement, for it is dressed as an infant in a long robe, a bonnet and long cloak, and proper under-garments, all beautifully made in knitting and all capable of taking off and putting on. Perhaps the work may be too difficult for a child to manage, but there are many mothers and aunts or kind friends, good knitters, who will take delight in dressing such a doll for a present; while, if two or three baby dolls are prepared for a bazaar or sale of work, they will elicit a perfect buzz of approbation and command ready sale.
Select a doll 13 inches or 14 inches high, one with a pretty, fair, babyish face.'
Reproduction baby doll 12'' (30 cm).
Clothes knitted in DMC Size 20 Cotton on 2 mm (14) needles, approximately 6 balls.
Cushion design from Knit One, Make One in Classic Knitted Cotton *by Furze Hewitt (Kangaroo Press).*

Row 1: K12, (sl 1, k1, psso, m1, k2 tog, k7) twice, sl 1, k1, psso, m1, k2 tog, k12 (47 sts).
Row 2: Purl.
Row 3: K11, (sl 1, k1, psso, m1, k1, m1, k2 tog, k5) twice, sl 1, k1, psso, m1, k1, m1, k2 tog, k11.
Row 4: Purl.
Row 5: K10, (sl 1, k1, psso, m1, k3, m1, k2 tog, k3) twice, sl 1, k1, psso, m1, k3, m1, k2 tog, k10.
Row 6: Purl.
Row 7: K9, (sl 1, k1, psso, m1, k5, m1, k2 tog, k1) twice, sl 1, k1, psso, m1, k5, m1, k2 tog, k9.
Row 8: Purl.
Knit 4 rows, decreasing 1 st at end of 4th row (46 sts).
Row 13: Sl 1, *m1, k2 tog, k1, repeat from * to end of row.
Row 14: Purl.
Row 15-20: Repeat Rows 13 and 14 3 times.
Row 21-24: Knit 4 rows (46 sts).
Repeat the 24 rows 4 times, decreasing to shape front thus:
Begin, and end, the 1st, 3rd, 5th and 7th rows with 2 sts less on account of the decreasing you are gradually making to shape front of robe. At the end of Rows 36 and 48 you will have 42 sts on needle.
Next repeat has 4 sts less at beginning and end of rows.
Next repeat has 6 sts less at beginning and end of rows.
Next repeat has 8 sts less at beginning and end of rows.
When you have worked nine insertions (108 rows), you will have (30 sts). Work next row as Row 13, omitting 1 k st at end of row. This forms perpendicular pattern of robe. Continue for 5'' (13 cm). Work 4 k rows, work row of holes, then k 2 rows.

Shape shoulders thus:
Row 1: K4 sts, turn.
Row 2: K4.
Row 3: Sl 1, m1, k2 tog, k1, turn.
Row 4: P4.
Knit 4 rows. Cast off.
Cast off 22 sts in centre of robe, k3, turn.
Row 1: K4.
Row 2: Sl 1, k1, m1, k2 tog, turn.
Row 3: P4.
Knit 4 rows. Cast off.

Back of robe

Cast on 139 sts.
Knit 5 rows.
Row 1: K7, *sl 1, k1, psso, m1, k2 tog, k7, repeat from * to end of row (127 sts).
Row 2: Purl.
Row 3: K6, *sl 1, k1, psso, m1, k1, m1, k2 tog, k5, repeat from * to last st, k1.

Row 4: Purl.
Row 5: K5, *sl 1, k1, psso, m1, k3, m1, k2 tog, k3, repeat from * to last 2 sts, k2.
Row 6: Purl.
Row 7: K4, *sl 1, k1, psso, m1, k5, m1, k2 tog, k1, repeat from * to last 3 sts, k3.
Row 8: Purl.
Knit 4 rows, decreasing 1 st at the end of 4th row (126 sts).
Row 13: Sl 1, *m1, k2 tog, k1, repeat from * to last 2 sts, m1, k2 tog.
Row 14: Purl.
Rows 15-20: Repeat last 2 rows 3 times.
Rows 21-24: Knit 4 rows.
These 24 rows correspond with pattern on front of robe. Proceed in st st until work measures 10'' (25 cm).
Next Row: K2 tog to end of row (63 sts).
Next Row: Purl.
Make row of holes: K3, *m1, k2 tog, k1, repeat from * to end of row.
Next Row: Purl.
Work in st st for 3'' (8 cm), knit 4 rows. Work row of holes as on front of robe. Knit 2 rows.
Shape shoulders on 4 sts as on front. Cast off until 4 shoulder sts remain. Work these as on front. Cast off. Sew front and back together, leaving space for armholes. Join shoulders. Edge bottom of robe with same lace as petticoat. The robe is trimmed with a narrower version of this lace.

Narrow lace

Cast on 7 sts.
Row 1: Sl 1, k2 tog, m1, k1, m1, k2 tog, m1, k1.
Row 2 and alternate rows: Knit.
Row 3: Sl 1, k2 tog, m1, k2, m1, k2 tog, m1, k1.
Row 5: Sl 1, k2 tog, m1, k3, m1, k2 tog, m1, k1.
Row 7: Sl 1, k2 tog, m1, k4, m1, k2 tog, m1, k1.
Row 9: Sl 1, k2 tog, m1, k5, m1, k2 tog, m1, k1,
Row 11: Sl 1, k2 tog, m1, k6, m1, k2 tog, m1, k1.
Row 12: Cast off 6 sts, k6.
Repeat Rows 1-12 until two pieces of lace are sufficiently long to reach from cast on sts of the front of robe to the shoulder strap and around the back of the armhole to form a lace sleeve. Sew straight edge of lace along the openwork panel of robe, as in illustration. Work lengths of chain (or use fine ribbon), thread through holes at neck and waist. The robe slips over doll's head, the ribbons tie at back.

Cloak

Cast on 66 sts.
Row 1: Knit.
Row 2: Purl.
Row 3: Knit.
Row 4: Purl.
Row 5: Knit.
Repeat Rows 1–5 until you have 23 raised and 22 depressed ribs. Cast off. The side that commences and ends with a raised rib is the right side of cloak.

Work an insertion for bottom of cloak thus:
Cast on 161 sts.
Work as the back of robe until you have completed the 1st 5 k rows, 8 pattern rows, 4 k rows, then cast off. Sew insertion to bottom of cloak. Knit lace as on robe. Make sufficient quantity to trim both fronts, and bottom, allowing ample fullness at corners. Knit a small length of lace, approx. 7 patterns, to go around the gathered neck edge to form a collar. Sew ribbon ties at neck and centre of cloak if desired.

Hat

Cast on 11 sts.
Row 1: Sl 1, (k1, p1) to end of row.
Work as above until the work measures 1¾" (4.5 cm).
Cast off.
Cast on 17 sts.
Work in moss st as above until the work measures 6½" (16.5 cm). Cast off.
Sew the strip of knitting around two sides of the back of hat. This forms head piece. Now work loop pattern to sew around front and back of hat.
Cast on 5 sts.
Row 1: Knit.
Row 2: Sl 1, insert needle in 2nd st while it remains in this position, pass the yarn 3 times round 2 fingers of L.H., and over point of needle, knit, drawing all threads through. Work 3rd and 4th sts in same way. K last st.
Row 3: Knit.
Repeat Rows 2 and 3 until length required to edge hat. Cast off. Sew neatly to head piece. Sew ribbons to tie under chin.

Pinafore: CAROL

Reproduction Bru 'Miranda' 18'' (46 cm) doll.
Over a simple black gown this doll is wearing a Victorian style pinafore. You will need 4 × 20 g balls of
DMC Blanc 5200 Cotton and a pair of 3 mm (11) needles.
Doll by Aileen Sellen, from the author's collection.

Front and back alike.
Cast on 168 sts.
Row 1: Knit.
Row 2 and alternate rows: Purl.
Row 3: *K6, m1, k2 tog, repeat from * to end of row.
Row 5: Knit.
Row 7: K2, *m1, k2 tog, k6, repeat from *, ending last repeat k4.
Row 8: Purl.
These 8 rows form the pattern. Continue in pattern until length desired, ending with Row 8.
Next Row (right side): *K2 tog, repeat from * to end of row (84 sts).
Next Row: Purl.
Continue thus:
Row 1: (K1, tbl, p1) 10 times, k7, (m1, k2 tog, k6) 4 times, m1, k2 tog, k3, (p1, k1, tbl) 10 times.
Row 2: (P1, k1, tbl) 10 times, p44, (k1, tbl, p1) 10 times.
Row 3: (K1, tbl, p1) 10 times, k44, (p1, k1, tbl) 10 times.
Row 4: As Row 2.
Row 5: (K1, tbl, p1) 10 times, k3, (m1, k2 tog, k6) 5 times, k1, (p1, k1, tbl) 10 times.
Row 6: As Row 2.
Row 7: Cast off 20 sts in rib, knit to last 20 sts, (p1, k1, tbl) 10 times.
Row 8: Cast off 20 sts in rib, purl to end (44 sts).
Continue in pattern thus:
Row 1 (right side): K1, *k6, m1, k2 tog, repeat from * to last 3 sts, k3.
Row 2 and every alternate row: Purl.
Row 3: Knit.
Row 5: K3, m1, k2 tog, * k6, m1, k2 tog, repeat from * to last 7 sts, k7.
Row 7: Knit.
Row 8: Purl.
These 8 rows form the pattern. Repeat these 8 rows 4 times, ending with Row 8. Length of pinafore can be adjusted here if desired.

Shape neck:
Next Row: K8, cast off 28 sts, k to end of row.
Work right side of neck.
Next Row: P to last 2 sts, p2 tog.

Next Row: K2 tog, k to end of row.
Repeat the last 2 rows twice. Cast off last 2 sts.
Work left side of neck. With wrong side of work facing join cotton to next st.
Next Row: P2 tog, purl to end.
Next Row: K to last 2 sts, k2 tog.
Repeat the last 2 rows twice. Cast off last 2 sts.

Lace hem edgings

Make 2.
Cast on 18 sts.
Foundation Row (wrong side): K6, p7, k5.
Commence pattern:
Row 1: Sl 1, k2, m1, k2 tog, k2, k2 tog, m1, k5, m1, k2 tog, (m1, k1) twice.
Row 2: K6, m1, k2 tog, p7, k2, m1, k2 tog, k1.
Row 3: Sl 1, k2, m1, k2 tog, k1, (k2 tog, m1) twice, k4, m1, k2 tog, (m1, k1) twice, k2.
Row 4: K8, m1, k2 tog, p7, k2, m1, k2 tog, k1.
Row 5: Sl 1, k2, m1, k2 tog, (k2 tog, m1) 3 times, k3, m1, k2 tog, (m1, k1) twice, k4.
Row 6: K10, m1, k2 tog, p7, k2, m1, k2 tog, k1.
Row 7: Sl 1, k2, m1, k2 tog, k1, (k2 tog, m1) twice, k4, m1, k2 tog, (m1, k1) twice, k6.
Row 8: Cast off 8 sts, k3, m1, k2 tog, p7, k2, m1, k2 tog, k1.
These 8 rows form pattern. Repeat until length desired.
Cast off.

Shoulder pieces

Make 2.
Work as given for lace hem edgings, ending with Row 8. Cast off.

To make up, lightly press work. Sew edgings to pinafore. Attach shoulder pieces. Use ribbon or cord to tie pinafore underarm.
Neck edge can be neatened with a simple crochet edge.

Lace-trimmed Dresses

BLYTHE

Reproduction Bru 22'' (56 cm).
A bloused and tucked dress transformed with finely knitted lace. For the wide collar, sleeves and skirt
edgings you will need approximately 4 × 20 g balls of DMC Blanc 5200 Cotton, size 100, and a pair of
1.25 needles. A length of ribbon to tie at neck. The doll wears a simple plaited head band.
Doll by Pat Blyth.

Collar

Cast on 53 sts.
Row 1: Sl 1, k1, k2 tog, m2, k2 tog, k5, k2 tog, m2, (k2 tog) twice, m2, k2 tog, k8, k2 tog, m2, (k2 tog) twice, m2, k2 tog, k5, k2 tog, m2, k2 tog, k2, k2 tog, m2, k2 tog, k3.
Row 2: (K5, p1) twice, k8, p1, k3, p1, k11, p1, k3, p1, k8, p1, k3.
Row 3: Sl 1, k3, k2 tog, m2, k2 tog, k5, k2 tog, m2, k2 tog, k12, k2 tog, m2, k2 tog, k5, k2 tog, m2, k2 tog, k6, k2 tog, m2, k2, inc in last st.
Row 4: K5, p1, k9, p1, k8, p1, k15, p1, k8, p1, k5.
Row 5: Sl 1, k1, k2 tog, m2, (k2 tog) twice, m2, k2 tog, k5, k2 tog, m2, k2 tog, k8, k2 tog, m2, k2 tog, k5, k2 tog, m2, k2 tog, k10, k2 tog, m2, k2, inc 1.
Row 6: K5, p1, k13, p1, k8, p1, k11, p1, k8, (p1, k3) twice.
Row 7: Sl 1, k3, k2 tog, m2, (k2 tog) twice, m2, k2 tog, k5, k2 tog, m2, k2 tog, k4, k2 tog, m2, k2 tog, k5, k2 tog, m2, k2 tog, k14, k2 tog, m2, k2, inc 1.
Row 8: K5, p1, k17, p1, k8, p1, k7, p1, k8, p1, k3, p1, k5.
Row 9: Sl 1, k1, k2 tog, m2, (k2 tog) twice, m2, (k2 tog) twice, m2, k2 tog, k5, k2 tog, m2, (k2 tog) twice, m2, k2 tog, k5, k2 tog, m2, k2 tog, k18, k2 tog, m2, k2, inc 1.
Row 10: K5, p1, k21, p1, k8, p1, k3, p1, k8, (p1, k3) 3 times.
Row 11: Sl 1, k3, k2 tog, m2, (k2 tog) twice, m2, (k2 tog) twice, m2, k2 tog, k5, k2 tog, m2, k2 tog, k5, k2 tog, m2, k2 tog, k22, k2 tog, m2, k3.
Row 12: K4, p1, k25, (p1, k8) twice, (p1, k3) twice, p1, k5.
Row 13: Sl 1, k1, k2 tog, m2, (k2 tog) twice, m2, (k2 tog) twice, m2, k2 tog, k5, k2 tog, m2, (k2 tog) twice, m2, k2 tog, k5, k2 tog, m2, k2 tog, k18, k2 tog, m2, (k2 tog) 3 times.
Row 14: K2 tog, k2, p1, k21, p1, k8, p1, k3, p1, k8, (p1, k3) 3 times.

Row 15: Sl 1, k3, k2 tog, m2, (k2 tog) twice, m2, k2 tog, k5, k2 tog, m2, k2 tog, k4, k2 tog, m2, k2 tog, k5, k2 tog, m2, k2 tog, k14, k2 tog, m2, (k2 tog) twice, k1.
Row 16: K2 tog, k2, p1, k17, p1, k8, p1, k7, p1, k8, p1, k3, p1, k5.
Row 17: Sl 1, k1, k2 tog, m2, (k2 tog) twice, m2, k2 tog, k5, k2 tog, m2, k2 tog, k8, k2 tog, m2, k2 tog, k5, k2 tog, m2, k2 tog, k10, k2 tog, m2, (k2 tog) twice, k1.
Row 18: K2 tog, k2, p1, k13, p1, k8, p1, k11, p1, k8, (p1, k3) twice.
Row 19: Sl 1, k3, k2 tog, m2, k2 tog, k5, k2 tog, m2, k2 tog, k12, k2 tog, m2, k2 tog, k5, k2 tog, m2, k2 tog, k6, k2 tog, m2, (k2 tog) twice, k1.
Row 20: K2 tog, k2, p1, k9, p1, k8, p1, k15, p1, k8, p1, k5.
Repeat Rows 1–20 until length desired, ending work on Row 2.

Edgings

Cast on 6 sts.
Row 1: M1, p2 tog, k3, k in f and b of last st.
Row 2: K5, m1, p2 tog.
Row 3: M1, p2 tog, k1, (m2, k2 tog) twice.
Row 4: (K2, p1) twice, k1, m1, p2 tog.
Row 5: M1, p2 tog, k7.
Row 6: Cast off 3 sts, k3, m1, p2 tog.
Repeat Rows 1–6 until length desired.

Antique A.M. 900.
Made in fine batiste, the dress has a rounded yoke and tucked skirt. The neck, sleeves and skirt edgings will require 2 balls DMC 5200 Size 20 Cotton and a pair of 2 mm (14) needles. The dress is embroidered in feather stitch using DMC Size 12 Cotton. The doll is wearing a bonnet from the Gossamer pattern, knitted in 3-ply cotton on size 2.75 needles (see page 21). Make ribbon rosettes as side trims. Tie ribbons under chin if desired.
Doll from author's collection.

TAMSIN

Skirt edging

Cast on 13 sts.
Row 1: Sl 1, k9, m2, k2 tog, k1.
Row 2: K3, p1, k10.
Row 3: Sl 1, k10, m2, k2 tog, k1.
Row 4: K3, p1, k11.
Row 5: Sl 1, k4, k2 tog, m2, k2 tog, k3, m2, k2 tog, k1.
Row 6: K3, p1, k5, p1, k6.
Row 7: Sl 1, k12, m2, k2 tog, k1.
Row 8: K3, p1, k13.
Row 9: Sl 1, k2, k2 tog, m2, (k2 tog) twice, m2, k2 tog, k3, m2, k2 tog, k1.
Row 10: K3, p1, k5, p1, k3, p1, k4.
Row 11: Sl 1, k11, k2 tog, m2, (k2 tog) twice.
Row 12: K3, p1, k13.
Row 13: Sl 1, k4, k2 tog, m2, k2 tog, k2, k2 tog, m2, (k2 tog) twice.
Row 14: K3, p1, k5, p1, k6.

Row 15: Sl 1, k9, k2 tog, m2, (k2 tog) twice.
Row 16: K3, p1, k11.
Row 17: Sl 1, k8, k2 tog, m2, (k2 tog) twice.
Row 18: K3, p1, k10.
Row 19: Sl 1, k7, k2 tog, m2, (k2 tog) twice.
Row 20: K3, p1, k9.
Repeat Rows 1–20 until length desired.

Sleeves

Cast on 6 sts.
Row 1: Sl 1, k1, m1, k2 tog, m2, k2.
Row 2: Sl 1, k2, p1, k4.
Row 3: Sl 1, k1, m1, k2 tog, k4.
Row 4: Cast off 2 sts, k5.
Repeat Rows 1–4 until length desired.

Neck edging

Use Foliage Lace (see page 75).

Knitted Doll: KLASINA
OF COCKINGTON GREEN

Doll back

Cast on 31 sts.
Row 1: Knit.
Row 2: Purl.
Row 3: (Inc 1, k14) twice, inc 1.
Work 3 rows st st.
Row 7: (Inc 1, k15) twice, inc 1.
Work 3 rows st st.
Row 11: (Inc 1, k17) twice, inc 1.
Work 3 rows st st.
Row 15: Inc 1, k19, inc 1, k18, inc 1.
Work 3 rows st st.
Row 19: (Inc 1, k20) twice, inc. 1.
Work 3 rows st st.
Row 23: Inc 1, k21, inc 1, k22, inc 1.
Work 5 rows st st.
Row 29: K2 tog, k21, k2 tog, k22, k2 tog.
Work 3 rows st st.
Row 33: (K2 tog, k20) twice, k2 tog.
Work 3 rows st st.
Row 37: K2 tog, k18, k2 tog, k19, k2 tog.
Work 3 rows st st.
Row 41: (K2 tog, k17) twice, k2 tog.
Work 3 rows st st.
Row 45: K2 tog, k15, k2 tog, k16, k2 tog.
Work 3 rows st st.
Row 49: (K2 tog, k14) twice, k2 tog.
Work 5 rows st st.
Row 55: Inc 1 each end of needle, and every 5th row
(45 sts).
Work 12 rows st st.
**Cast off 13 sts at beginning of next 2 rows (neck
shaping).
K2 tog each end of next row.
Purl one row.

Head

Cast on 2 sts at beginning of next 8 rows.
Work 2 rows st st.
Inc 1 at each end of every 5th row (41 sts).
Purl 1 row.

Work 10 rows st st.
K2 tog at each end of next and every 5th row (33 sts).
Cast off 3 sts at beginning of next 4 rows.
Cast off.

Front

Cast on 31 sts.
Row 1: Knit.
Row 2: Purl.
Inc 1 each end of next and every 5th row (43 sts).
Work 5 rows st st.
K2 tog at each end of next and every 5th row (31 sts).
Work 5 rows st st.
Inc 1, k8, inc 1, k11, inc 1, k8, inc 1.
Work 3 rows st st.
Inc 1, k10, inc 1, k11, inc 1, k10, inc 1.
Work 3 rows st st.
Inc 1, k11, inc 1, k13, inc 1, k11, inc 1.
Work 3 rows st st.
(Inc 1, k13) 3 times, inc 1.
Work 3 rows st st.
Inc 1, k14, k2 tog, k13, k2 tog, k14, inc 1.
Work 3 rows st st.
Inc 1, k14, k2 tog, k13, k2 tog, k14, inc 1.
Work 3 rows st st.
Inc 1, k14, k2 tog, k13, k2 tog, k14, inc 1.
Work 3 rows st st.
Inc 1, k14, k2 tog, k13, k2 tog, k14, inc 1.
Work 3 rows st st.
K15, k2 tog, k13, k2 tog, k15 (45 sts).
Purl 1 row.
Work 8 rows st st.
Continue from ** as back of doll.

Legs

Make 2.
Cast on 30 sts.
Work 44 rows st st, approx. 3½'' (9 cm).
Shape as follows:
Row 1: Inc 1 at beginning of row.
Work 3 rows st st.

*Klasina was created especially for this book by Kathy Grin. She is 21'' (53 cm) tall, and makes a
charming gift.*
*To make her, you will require a quantity of 3-ply unbleached knitting cotton. This soft yarn gives the
appearance of calico. Dark yarn in a small quantity for shoes. Small piece of wadding for lining face,
polyester filling, small buttons for eyes (embroider the eyes if the doll is intended for a small child),
embroidery thread for details of face, a wig (obtainable from doll studios), pair of 2 mm (14) needles.
For Klasina's dress and underwear lace, you will need approximately 2 × 50 g balls of 4-ply cotton,
2 mm and 2.25 needles, 4 small white buttons.*

Row 5: Knit, inc 1 in last st.
Work 3 rows st st.
Continue until there are 38 sts on needle.
K2 tog, k to end of row.
Work 3 rows st st.
K to last 2 sts, k2 tog.
Work 3 rows st st.
Continue until there are 32 sts on needle.
K2 tog, k28, k2 tog.
Purl 1 row.
Break off yarn. Slip 11 sts on holder, k8, sl 11 sts on another holder, turn.
Work 11 rows st st on these 8 sts for instep.

Shoes

Make 2.
With dark yarn, pick up and knit 11 sts from stitch holder, pick up 11 sts along instep, k8 sts on needle, pick up 11 sts from instep, knit 11 sts from stitch holder (52 sts).
Knit 10 rows.
Shape shoes thus:
Row 1: (K2 tog, k23) twice, k2 tog.
Row 2: K4, k2 tog, k13, k2 tog, k7, k2 tog, k13, k2 tog, k4 (45 sts).
Row 3: Knit.
Row 4: K3, k2 tog, k12, k2 tog, k7, k2 tog, k12, k2 tog, k3.
Row 5: Knit.
Row 6: K2, k2 tog, k33, k2 tog, k2 (39 sts).
Row 7: Knit.
Row 8: K1, k2 tog, k12, k2 tog, k5, k2 tog, k12, k2 tog, k1.
Row 9: Knit.
Row 10: K2 tog, k12, k2 tog, k3, k2 tog, k12, k2 tog.
Row 11: Knit.
Row 12: K2 tog, k11, k2 tog, k1, k2 tog, k11, k2 tog.
Cast off.

Arms

Make 4, 2 in reverse.
Cast on 6 sts.
Work in st st for 2 rows.
Inc 1 at each end of Rows 3, 5 and 7.
Inc 1 at beginning of Row 8 (at end for reverse).
Inc 1 at each end of Row 9.
Inc 1 at beginning of Row 10 (at end for reverse).
Knit Row 11.
Dec 1 st at beginning of Row 12 (at end for reverse).
Knit Row 13.
Dec both ends of Row 14.

Knit Rows 15 and 16.
Dec both ends Row 17.
Work 3 rows st st.
Inc 1 each end of Rows 21, 23 and 25 (17 sts).
Work 60 rows st st, approx. 5'' (13 cm).
Cast off 3 sts at beginning of next and every alternate 4 rows, making dec at thumb side.
Cast off.

Assembling doll

Lightly press on wrong side, line face with thin wadding. Sew front to back along side and head, leaving bottom open. Stuff with filling, making sure to fill head and neck firmly.
Sew bottom seam. Embroider face and eyes. Klasina has button eyes, but for a young child embroidered eyes would be safer.
Arms: Sew together matching thumbs. Fill lower arm to elbow firmly. Sew in dimple with darning needle, fill top of arm lightly. Attach arms to body with top seam approx. ¼'' (1 cm) behind shoulder seam.
Legs: Sew back seam and shoe. Fill firmly to knee. Sew dimple through leg. Lightly fill top of leg, so that Klasina can sit. Sew legs to body.
Attach a wig to the head, or embroider hair.

Dress

Cast on 171 sts. Knit 3 rows.
Row 1: K1, *m1, k3, sl 1, k2 tog, psso, k3, m1, k1, repeat from * to end or row.
Row 2: Purl.
Row 3: As Row 1.
Row 4: Knit.
These 4 rows form the pattern. Work approx. 10'' (25 cm), adjusting skirt length to your requirements.
K2 tog across next row (86 sts).
Dec 11 sts evenly across next ribbed row.
Change to 2 mm needles.
Work 4 rows in k1, p1, rib (knit sts worked through back of loops).
Change to 2.25 needles.
K57, place next 18 sts on holder, turn, work all knit sts tbl, purl 39 sts, place remaining sts on holder.
Work 5 rows st st.
Cast off 2 sts at beginning of next 4 rows.
Work 10 rows st st.
Next row k11, cast off 9 sts, k11.
Purl.
Cast off 2 sts, knit.
Purl.
Cast off 1 st, knit.

Work 3 rows st st.
Cast off.
Work other shoulder to correspond.

Sleeves

Make 2.
Cast on 30 sts using 2 mm needles.
K1, p1, rib 5 rows.
Next row, k1, p1 in every st (60 sts).
Change to 2.25 needles. Work approx. 5½'' (14 cm) in skirt pattern. Next row inc 1 st in middle of row (61 sts).
Dec 3 sts at beginning of next 6 rows.
Next row k2 tog to end of row.
Next row p2 tog to end of row.
Cast off.

To make up dress:
Press lightly on wrong side of work.
Sew back seam to ½'' (1.5 cm) below waist band. Right side of work facing, pick up 23 sts from each side of back opening (46 sts).
Knit 3 rows.
Next row *k4, m1, k2 tog, repeat from * twice (3 buttonholes), knit to end of row.

Knit next row.
Cast off.
Sew shoulder seams. With right side of work facing, using 2 mm needles, pick up and knit 38 sts. Work 2 rows in rib.
Next row, make buttonhole on same level as the others.
Work 2 rows in rib.
Cast off.
Sew sleeves into armholes. Sew up side and sleeve seams.
Sew on buttons to correspond with buttonholes.

Lace edging for underwear

Cast on 14 sts.
Row 1: K3, m1, k2 tog, k1, k2 tog, k1, m1, k1, m1, k4 (15 sts).
Row 2: K4, m1, k3, m1, k2 tog, k3, m1, k2 tog, k1 (16 sts).
Row 3: K3, m1, (k2 tog) twice, m1, k5, m1, k4 (17 sts).
Row 4: Cast off 3 sts, m1, (k1, k2 tog) twice, k1, m1, k3, m1, k2 tog, k1 (14 sts).
Row 5: K3, m1, k2 tog, k2, m1, k2 tog, k1, k2 tog, m1, k2 (14 sts).
Row 6: K3, m1, sl 1, k2 tog, psso, m1, k5, m1, k2 tog, k1 (14 sts).
Repeat Rows 1–6 until length desired.
Cast off. Press lightly. Sew to underwear.

Dress: ONDINE

A delicate design in DMC 100 Cotton. Knitted on 2 mm (14) needles. The bodice of the dress was created from two lengths of fan lace. Using 100 Cotton and Size 20 needles knit two flowers (as illustrated on page 70). These form the bust line. Sew the lengths of lace to the skirt top to form sleeves. Ribbons can be used to adjust skirt fullness. The doll illustrated has crocheted wings, however, by knitting one repeat of the pattern for each wing, you can form similar ones. The wings require a light spray of starch. Attach the wings to the doll with tiny sts. Ondine wears a tiny circlet of beads. Using large needles, and the finest of threads, a diaphanous effect is achieved. Why not dress a fairy doll for your Christmas Tree?
Doll created by Ellen Watt.

Cast on 38 sts.

Work 2 foundation rows thus:

Row 1: Sl 1, k2, m1, k2 tog, k6, m1, k2 tog, k1, (m1, k2 tog) 6 times, k12.

Row 2: K27, m1, k2 tog, k6, m1, k2 tog, k1.

Now continue lace pattern:

Row 1: Sl 1, k2, m1, (k2 tog) twice, m2, sl 1, k1, psso, k2, m1, k2 tog, k19, k2 tog, m1, k2 tog, m3, k1, inc in last st.

Row 2: K4, p1, k25, m1, k2 tog, k2, p1, k3, m1, k2 tog, k1.

Row 3: Sl 1, k2, m1, k2 tog, k6, m1, k2 tog, k17, k2 tog, (m1, k2 tog) twice, k5.

Row 4: Cast off 2 sts, k26, m1, k2 tog, k6, m1, k2 tog, k1.

Row 5: Sl 1, k2, m1, (k2 tog) twice, m2, sl 1, k1, psso, k2, m1, k2 tog, k15, k2 tog, (m1, k2 tog) 3 times, m3, k1, inc in last st.

Row 6: As Row 2.

Row 7: Sl 1, k2, m1, k2 tog, k6, m1, k2 tog, k13, k2 tog, (m1, k2 tog) 4 times, k5.

Row 8: As Row 4.

Row 9: Sl 1, k2, m1, (k2 tog) twice, m2, sl 1, k1, psso, k2, m1, k2 tog, k11, k2 tog, (m1, k2 tog) 5 times, m3, k1, inc in last st.

Row 10: As Row 2.

Row 11: Sl 1, k2, m1, k2 tog, k6, m1, k2 tog, k9, k2 tog, (m1, k2 tog) 6 times, k5.

Row 12: As Row 4.

Row 13: Sl 1, k2, m1, (k2 tog) twice, m2, sl 1, k1, psso, k2, m1, k2 tog, k7, k2 tog, (m1, k2 tog) 7 times, m3, k1, inc in last st.

Row 14: As Row 2.

Row 15: Sl 1, k2, m1, k2 tog, k6, m1, k2 tog, k5, k2 tog, (m1, k2 tog) 8 times, k5.

Row 16: As Row 4.

Row 17: Sl 1, k2, m1, (k2 tog) twice, m2, sl 1, k1, psso, k2, m1, k2 tog, k3, k2 tog, (m1, k2 tog) 9 times, m3, k1, inc in last st.

Row 18: As Row 2.

Row 19: Sl 1, k2, m1, k2 tog, k6, m1, k2 tog, k6, (m1, k2 tog) 8 times, k6.

Row 20: Cast off 3 sts, k26, m1, k2 tog, k6, m1, k2 tog, k1.

Row 21: Sl 1, k2, m1, (k2 tog) twice, m2, sl 1, k1, psso, k2, m1, k2 tog, k8, (m1, k2 tog) 7 times, m3, k2 tog, inc in last st.

Row 22: As Row 2.

Row 23: Sl 1, k2, m1, k2 tog, k6, m1, k2 tog, k10, (m1, k2 tog) 6 times, k6.

Row 24: As Row 20.

Row 25: Sl 1, k2, m1, (k2 tog) twice, m2, sl 1, k1, psso, k2, m1, k2 tog, k12, (m1, k2 tog) 5 times, m3, k2 tog, inc in last st.

Row 26: As Row 2.

Row 27: Sl 1, k2, m1, k2 tog, k6, m1, k2 tog, k14, (m1, k2 tog) 4 times, k6.

Row 28: As Row 20.

Row 29: Sl 1, k2, m1, (k2 tog) twice, m2, sl 1, k1, psso, k2, m1, k2 tog, k16, (m1, k2 tog) 3 times, m3, k2 tog, inc in last st.

Row 30: As Row 2.

Row 31: Sl 1, k2, m1, k2 tog, k6, m1, k2 tog, k18, (m1, k2 tog) twice, k6.

Row 32: As Row 20.

Row 33: Sl 1, k2, m1, (k2 tog) twice, m2, sl 1, k1, psso, k2, m1, k2 tog, k20, m1, k2 tog, m3, k2 tog, inc in last st.

Row 34: As Row 2.

Row 35: Sl 1, k2, m1, k2 tog, k6, m1, k2 tog, k1, (m1, k2 tog) 6 times, k15.

Row 36: Cast off 3 sts, k26, m1, k2 tog, k6, m1, k2 tog, k1.

Repeat Rows 1–36 until length desired. Cast off.

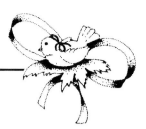

Granny Bonnet: THEA

Granny bonnet knitted in Gyps'Anny yarn on 4 mm (8) needles. One ball of yarn. The bonnet illustrated has seven tiny ribbon bows along the centre of the Van Dyke strip.

The bonnet consists of two strips of Van Dyke edgings, in two widths.

Wide strip

Cast on 10 sts.
Row 1: M1, knit to end of row.
Rows 2-20: Repeat Row 1 until you have 30 sts.
Row 21: M1, (k2 tog) twice. Knit to end of row.
Repeat Row 21 19 times (10 sts).
Continue until there are 6 points on each side of the strip. Cast off.

Narrow strip

Cast on 10 sts.
Work as above until there are 20 sts instead of 30 sts.

Work from Row 21 until 10 sts remain. Continue until there are 6 points on each side of the strip. Cast off.

To assemble bonnet you will need a length of ribbon long enough to go from ear to ear of doll, allowing sufficient to tie under chin in a generous bow.
Mark the measurement of your doll's head from ear to ear in centre of ribbon. Run a gathering thread down the centre of the wide strip. Sew the gathered strip to the marks on ribbon (adjust gathers before stitching in place) and sew down centre of strip.
The narrow strip is gathered and placed on top of the wide strip. Carefully ease the gathers to make sure you have an even fullness and stitch down middle through all thicknesses.
Sew a length of matching ribbon at back of bonnet to hide the stitches.
The bonnet size can be varied by adjusting the number of Van Dykes worked, or by using a different thread.

Flounce for Collar, Cuffs and Bonnet: DOLLY PENTREATH

A character doll 26'' (66 cm) high.

Dolly Pentreath is wearing a Granny bonnet knitted in black. Instead of tiny bows, as on page 50, the trim is wide sheer ribbon, tied in a generous bow under the chin. This was fashionable in the 1870s. The flounce and cuffs were knitted on 2 mm (14) needles, the collar on 1.25 (18) needles. Approximately 8 × 20 g balls of DMC Size 30 Cotton in Shade 437. The skirt flounce is scattered with tiny bows of knitted cord.

Doll by Ellen Watt.

Cinnamon circles

Cast on 25 sts.

Row 1: Sl 1, k2, p10, m1, sl 1, k1, psso, k3, k2 tog, m1, k3, m1, k2.

Row 2: M1, k2 tog, k21, turn, leaving 3 sts on L.H. needle.

Row 3: P11, m1, sl 1, k1, psso, k1, k2 tog, m1, k5, m1, k2.

Row 4: M1, k2 tog, k22, turn, leaving 3 sts on L.H. needle.

Row 5: P12, m1, sl 1, k2 tog, psso, m1, sl 1, k1, psso, k2 tog, m3, k2 tog, k1, m1, k2.

Row 6: M1, k2 tog, k4, p1, k21.

Row 7: Sl 1, k12, k2 tog, m1, k3, m1, sl 1, k1, psso, k3, k2 tog, m1, k2 tog, k1.

Row 8: M1, k2 tog, k11, p11, turn, leaving 3 sts on L.H. needle.

Row 9: K9, k2 tog, m1, k5, m1, sl 1, k1, psso, k1, k2 tog, m1, k2 tog, k1.

Row 10: M1, k2 tog, k11, p10, turn, leaving 3 sts on L.H. needle.

Row 11: K8, k2 tog, m1, sl 1, k1, psso, k2 tog, m3, k2 tog, k1, m1, sl 1, k2 tog, psso, m1, k2 tog, k1.

Row 12: M1, k2 tog, k6, p1, k4, p9, k3.

Repeat Rows 1–12 until length desired.

Three Collars

The three collars illustrated were knitted in DMC Size 20 Cotton.
Berry, at the top, was knitted on 2.75 (12) needles.
Goffered, in the centre, was knitted on 2 (14) needles.
Snow Flutes, at the bottom of the picture, was knitted on 1.25 (18) needles.
2 × 20 g balls for each collar.
Trim as you wish. Collars can be fastened at the back if preferred to give a yoke-like effect.

BERRY COLLAR

Cast on 23 sts.
Row 1: K20, m2, k2 tog, k1.
Row 2: K3, (k1, p1) in m2 of previous row, k19, turn, leaving 1 st on needle.
Row 3: K23.
Row 4: K22, turn, leaving 2 sts on needle.
Row 5: K16, (m2, k2 tog) twice, m2, k2.
Row 6: K3, p1, (k2, p1) twice, k15, turn, leaving 3 sts on needle.
Row 7: K25.
Row 8: K24, turn, leaving 4 sts on needle.

Row 9: K10, k2 tog, m2, k2 tog, k3, (m2, k2 tog) 3 times, k1.
Row 10: K3, (p1, k2) twice, p1, k5, p1, k10, turn, leaving 5 sts on needle.
Row 11: K26.
Row 12: Cast off 8 sts, k16, turn, leaving 6 sts on needle.
Row 13: K14, m2, k2 tog, k1.
Row 14: K3, p1, k13, turn, leaving 7 sts on needle.
Row 15: K17.
Row 16: K16, turn, leaving 8 sts on needle.
Row 17: K10, (m2, k2 tog) twice, m2, k2.
Row 18: K3, (p1, k2) twice, p1, k9, turn, leaving 9 sts on needle.

Row 19: K19.

Row 20: K18, turn, leaving 10 sts on needle.

Row 21: K4, k2 tog, m2, k2 tog, k3, (m2, k2 tog) 3 times, k1.

Row 22: K3, (p1, k2) twice, p1, k5, p1, k4, turn, leaving 11 sts on needle.

Row 23: K20.

Row 24: Cast off 8 sts, k10, (m1, k2 tog) 6 times (23 sts).

Repeat Rows 1–24 9 times, cast off, press lightly.

GOFFERED COLLAR

Cast on 29 sts.

Row 1: K5, p16, (m1, k2 tog) 3 times, m1, k2.

Row 2: K25, turn.

Row 3: P17, (m1, k2 tog) 3 times, m1, k2.

Row 4: K26, turn.

Row 5: K18, (m1, k2 tog) 3 times, m1, k2.

Row 6: K9, p18, turn.

Row 7: K1, (m1, k2 tog) 12 times, m1, k2.

Row 8: K9, p19, k5.

Row 9: Knit.

Row 10: Cast off 4 sts, knit to end of row.

Repeat Rows 1–10 until length desired. Cast off.

SNOW FLUTES COLLAR

Cast on 29 sts.

Row 1: K5, p16, (m1, k2 tog) 3 times, m1, k2.

Row 2: K25, turn.

Row 3: P17, (m1, k2 tog) 3 times, m1, k2.

Row 4: K26, turn.

Row 5: K18, (m1, k2 tog) 3 times, m1, k2.

Row 6: K9, p18, turn.

Row 7: K19, (m1, k2 tog) 3 times, m1, k2.

Row 8: K9, p19, k5.

Row 9: Knit.

Row 10: Cast off 4 sts, knit to end of row.

Repeat Rows 1–10 until length desired. Cast off.

Reproduction Bru 22'' (56 cm) doll, wearing the Goffered collar.

Collar and Cuffs: RODERICK

Reproduction doll dressed in brown velvet.
The collar and cuffs require 2 × 20 g balls Cotton Ecru, Size 60, and 1.25 (18) needles. The fine knitting with the picot cast-off makes an ideal lace for the suit.
Doll by Ellen Watt.

Collar

Cast on 111 sts.
Row 1: *P7, k1, repeat from * to last 7 sts, p7.
Row 2: *K7, p1, repeat from * to last 7 sts, k7.
Row 3: *P7, m1, k1, m1, repeat from * to last 7 sts, p7.
Row 4: *K7, p3, repeat from * to last 7 sts, k7.
Row 5: *P7, m1, k3, m1, repeat from * to last 7 sts, p7.
Row 6: *K7, p5, repeat from * to last 7 sts, k7.
Row 7: *P7, m1, k5, m1, repeat from * to last 7 sts, p7.
Row 8: *K7, p7, repeat from * to last 7 sts, k7.
Row 9: *P7, m1, k7, m1, repeat from * to last 7 sts, p7.
Row 10: *K7, p9, repeat from * to last 7 sts, k7.
Row 11: *P7, m1, k9, m1, repeat from * to last 7 sts, p7.
Row 12: *K7, p11, repeat from * to last 7 sts, k7.
Row 13: *P7, m1, k11, m1, repeat from * to last 7 sts, p7.
Row 14: *K7, p13, repeat from * to last 7 sts, k7.
Row 15: *P7, m1, k13, m1, repeat from * to last 7 sts, p7.

Row 16: *K7, p15, repeat from * to last 7 sts, k7.
Row 17: *P7, m1, k15, m1, repeat from * to last 7 sts, p7.
Row 18: *K7, p17, repeat from * to last 7 sts, k7.
Row 19: *P7, m1, k17, m1, repeat from * to last 7 sts, p7.
Row 20: *K7, p19, repeat from * to last 7 sts, k7.
Cast off using picot method.
*Cast on 2 sts, cast off 4 sts, sl st used to cast off from R.H. needle to L.H. needle, repeat from * to end of row. Cast off.

Cuffs

Cast on 55 sts.
Proceed as for collar instructions.

Trimmed Hat: SARAH

Hat worn by a Limited Edition doll created by Kaye Wiggs.
Lace hatband knitted in DMC 40 cotton on 1.25 needles. Launceston lace pattern, page 75.
Hat brim edged with Sarah pattern, using DMC 100 Cotton on size 20 needles.
Only a small quantity of yarn used.

Cast on 7 sts.
Row 1: Knit.
Row 2: Purl.
Row 3: Sl 1, purlwise, k2, m1, k2 tog, m2, k2 tog.
Row 4: M1, k2, p1, k2, m1, k2 tog, k1.
Row 5: Sl 1, purlwise, k2, m1, k2 tog, k4.
Row 6: K6, m1, k2 tog, k1.
Row 7: Sl 1, purlwise, k2, m1, k2 tog, m2, k2 tog, m2, k2 tog.
Row 8: (K2, p1) twice, k2, m1, k2 tog, k1.

Row 9: Sl 1, purlwise, k2, m1, k2 tog, k6.
Row 10: K8, m1, k2 tog, k1.
Row 11: Sl 1, purlwise, k2, m1, k2 tog, (m2, k2 tog) 3 times.
Row 12: (K2, p1) 3 times, k2, m1, k2 tog, k1.
Row 13: Sl 1, purlwise, k2, m1, k2 tog, k9.
Row 14: Cast off 7 sts, k4, including st used in casting off, m1, k2 tog, k1.
Repeat Rows 3-14 until length desired. Cast off.

Petticoats and Vest

These dainty petticoats were knitted in DMC 20 Cotton on 2.75 (12) needles. Approximately one ball for each petticoat. You will need ribbon to thread through the holes. Use a contrasting colour if desired. A basic vest pattern to wear with the petticoats has been included.

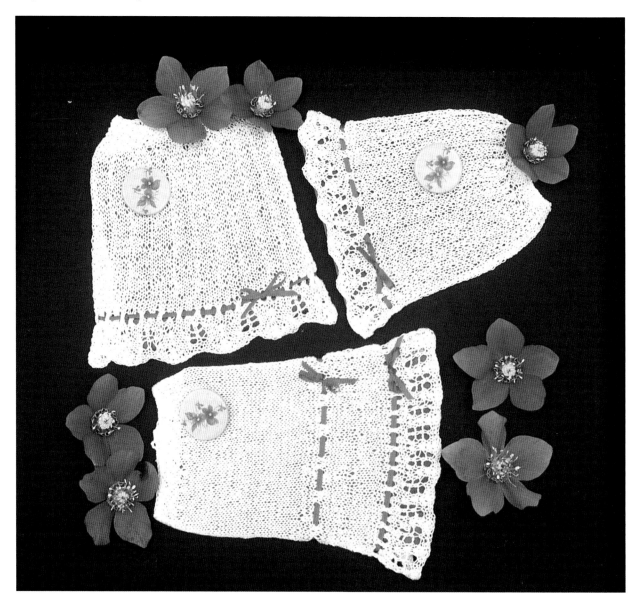

FLUTE PETTICOAT

Cast on 122 sts.
Row 1: Knit.
Row 2: Purl.
Row 3: Knit.

Row 4: Sl 1, k1, *m1, k3, sl 1, k2 tog, psso, k3, m1, k1, repeat from * to end of row.
Row 5: Purl.
Row 6: Sl 1, k2, *m1, k2, sl 1, k2 tog, psso, k2, m1, k3, repeat from * to last 2 sts, k2.
Row 7: Purl.

Row 8: Sl 1, k3, *m1, k1, sl 1, k2 tog, psso, k1, m1, k5, repeat from * to last 3 sts, k3.
Row 9: Purl.
Row 10: Sl 1, k2 tog, m2, *m1, sl 1, k2 tog, psso, m1, k2, sl 1, k2 tog, psso, k2, repeat from * to last 4 sts, k4 (99 sts on needle).
Row 11: Purl.
Row 12: Purl.
Row 13: Knit.
Row 14: Purl.
Row 15: Purl.
Row 16: K3, *m1, k2 tog, k1, repeat from * to end of row.
Row 17: Purl.
Row 18: Purl.
Row 19: Knit.
Row 20: Purl.
Row 21 (wrong side of work): P30, p2 tog, p35, p2 tog, p30 (97 sts).
Right side of petticoat—proceed as follows:
Row 1: Sl 1, k1, p1, *k3, p1, repeat from * to end of row, k2.
Row 2: Sl 1, purlwise, *k3, p1, repeat from * to end of row.
Repeat these two rows 23 times or till the length desired is reached.
Decrease for the waist:
Row 1: K2 tog, p1, *k3 tog, p1, repeat from * to last 2 sts, k2 tog (49 sts).
Row 2: Sl 1, (k1, p1) to end of row.
Row 3: Sl 1, (p1, k1) to end of row.
Knit 4 rows.
Row 8: Knit to last 4 sts, m1, k2 tog, k2, forming buttonhole.
Knit 3 rows.
Cast off with wrong side facing you. Press petticoat. Join back seam to within 1'' (2.5 cm) of waist. Sew on small button.

FANCY PETTICOAT

Cast on 110 sts.
Row 1: Knit.
Row 2: Purl.
Row 3: Knit.
Row 4: Sl 1, k1, *m1, k1, sl 1, k2 tog, psso, k1, m1, k1, repeat from * to end of row.
Row 5: Purl.
Repeat Rows 4 and 5 twice.
Row 10: *P4, p2 tog, repeat from * to last 2 sts, p2 (92 sts).
Row 11: Knit.
Row 12: Purl.
Row 13: Purl.

Row 14: Sl 1, k1, *m1, k2 tog, repeat from * to end of row (92 sts).
Continue thus:
Work 2 rows in purl, knit one row, decrease 2 sts along this row by k2 tog twice at even distance (90 sts); purl 2 rows.
Row 20: *K5, (p1, k1) twice, p1, repeat from * to end of row.
Row 21: Sl 1, *k1, (p1 k1) twice, p5, repeat from * to last 4 sts, p4.
Row 22: K3, *(p1, k1) twice, p1, k5, repeat from * to last 2 sts, k2.
Row 23: P3, *(k1, p1) twice, k1, p5, repeat from * to last 2 sts, p2.
Row 24: Sl 1, *(p1, k1) twice, p1, k5, repeat from * to last 4 sts, k4.
Row 25: P5, *(k1, p1) twice, k1, repeat from * to end of row.
Row 26: *(K1, p1) twice, k5, p1, repeat from * to end of row.
Row 27: *P1, k1, p5, k1, p1, k1, repeat from * to end of row.
Row 28: *K1, p1, k5, p1, k1, p1, repeat from * to end of row.
Work 2 purl rows, 1 knit row, 2 purl rows.
Row 34: Sl 1, k1, *m1, k2 tog, repeat from * to end of row.
Work 2 purl rows, 1 knit row.
Row 38: P6, *p2 tog, p9, repeat from * to last 7 sts, p2 tog, p5 (82 sts).
Row 39: Purl.
Continue in st st for 36 rows, or length desired.
Shape waist thus:
K1, k2 tog, alternately 4 times, k2, k2 tog, k2, alternately 14 times, k2 tog, k1, alternately 4 times (60 sts). Knit 9 rows, working buttonhole in 4th row. Cast off.
Sew up back seam, leaving space for opening. Sew button on waistband.

SCALLOPS PETTICOAT

Cast on 122 sts.
Row 1: Knit.
Row 2: Purl.
Row 3: Knit.
Row 4: Sl 1, k1, *m1, k4, sl 1, k2 tog, psso, k4, m1, k1, repeat from * to end of row.
Row 5: Purl.
Repeat last 2 rows twice.
Row 10: P6, *p3 tog, p9, repeat from * to last 8 sts, p3 tog, p5 (102 sts).
Row 11: Knit.
Row 12: Purl.
Row 13: Purl.

Row 14: Sl 1, k1, *m1, k2 tog, repeat from * to end of row.
Row 15: Purl.
Row 16: Purl.
Row 17: Knit.
Row 18: Purl.
Row 19: Purl (102 sts); edging completed.

Commence body of petticoat:
Row 1: Sl 1, k1, *p4, k1, repeat from * to end of row.
Row 2: Sl 1, *k4, p1, repeat from * to last st, k1.
Row 3: Knit.
Row 4: Sl 1, *k4, p1, repeat from * to last st, k1.
Row 5: Sl 1, k1, *p4, k1, repeat from * to end of row.
Row 6: Purl.
Repeat Rows 1–6 7 times.
Adjust length of garment if required.
Row 49: Sl 1, k1, *k2 tog, sl 1, k1, psso, k1, repeat from * to end of row (62 sts).
Row 50: Knit.
Row 51: Sl 1, (k10, k2 tog) twice, k13, (k2 tog, k10) twice (58 sts).
Knit 3 rows.

Row 55: Knit to last 3 sts, draw last st but one over last st, k1, drawn another st over, k2.
Row 56: K3, cast on 2 sts (to replace the two sts cast off to form buttonhole), knit to end of row.
Knit 3 rows.
Cast off. Sew up back seam, leaving opening for placket, sew button on waistband.

VEST

Cast on 60 sts.
Work in k2, p2 rib for approx. 4¾'' (12 cm) or length required.
K12, cast off 36 sts, k12.
Work in rib on these 12 sts for approx. 2¾'' (7 cm).
Join cotton and work the other 12 sts for the same length, then k12, cast on 36 sts, k12, continue in rib for other side of vest. Sew side seams leaving opening for armholes.
Crochet around neck and armholes, working 2 dc, 3 ch. Fasten off. Make crochet chain long enough to thread through holes at neck and to tie in bow at front.

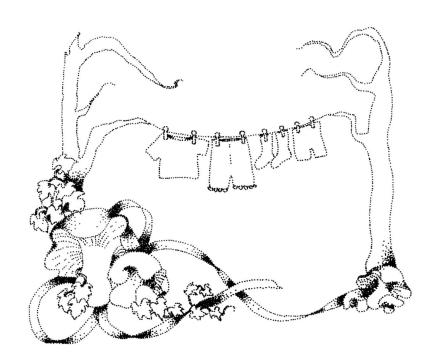

Rose White Underwear

The unadorned garments were created for this book. The designer has simplified the underwear, eliminating many of the curves and awkward angles found in dolls' patterns. Rose White samples made for this book were made in the traditional fashion with hand-sewn seams and tucks. The pattern sheets are available in eight sizes—a basic lingerie set for all your dolls. Information on Rose White patterns can be found in the list of suppliers.

Any of the edgings in this book would be suitable for trimming these tiny garments. Traditional embroidery, such as fine feather stitching, would add a finishing touch.

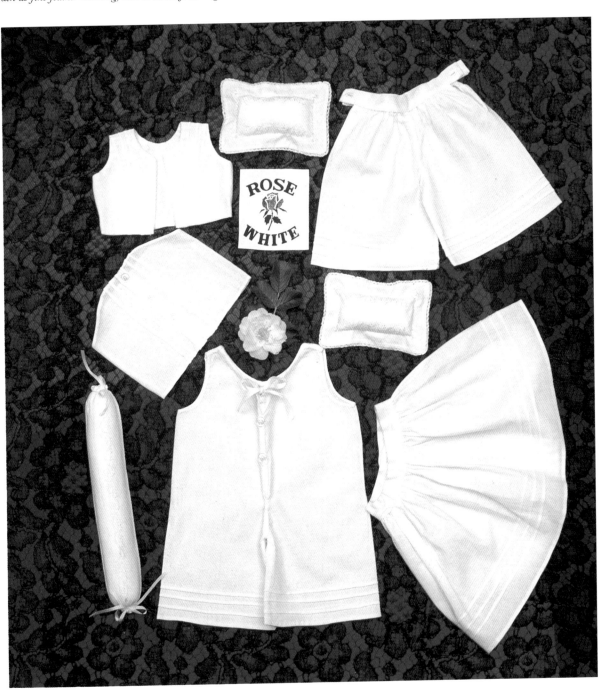

Socks

Four pairs of lacy socks knitted in DMC 20 Cotton using 2 mm (14) needles. These dainty socks make an ideal gift for a doll lover.

SOCK 1

Cast on 41 sts.
Work in k1, p1, rib for 10 rows.
Pattern:
Row 1: K4, *m1, sl 1, k2 tog, psso, m1, k3, repeat from * to last st, k1.
Row 2: Purl.
Row 3: K1, *m1, sl 1, k2 tog, psso, m1, k3, repeat from * to last 4 sts, m1, sl 1, k2 tog, psso, m1, k1.
Row 4: Purl.
Repeat Rows 1–4 9 times or adjust to length desired.
Shape heel thus:
K12, turn, sl 1, purlwise, purl to end of row.
K11, turn, sl 1, purlwise, purl to end of row.
Continue decreasing 1 st until you have worked k6, turn, sl 1, purlwise, purl to end of row.
Reverse heel thus:
K6, pick up loop from row below, knit it with next st

on L.H. needle, turn, sl 1 purlwise, purl to end.
Continue knitting 1 extra st with loop until all 12 sts are on needle.
Knit across all sts, inc once in 21st st (42 sts).
Work other side of heel thus:
Row 1: P12, turn, sl 1, knit to end of row.
Row 2: P11, turn, sl 1, knit to end of row.
Continue working 1 st less until you have worked p6, turn, sl 1, knit to end of row.
Reverse heel:
P6, pick up loop from row below and purl it with the next st on L.H. needle, turn, sl 1, k to end of row.
Continue this way, purling 1 extra st with loop until all 12 sts are on needle.
Work 12 rows st st.
Shape toe thus:
Row 1: *K5, k2 tog, repeat from * to end of row.

Row 2: Purl.
Row 3: *K4, k2 tog, repeat from * to end of row.
Decrease this way until 12 sts remain. Thread yarn through the sts, and sew up back seam.

SOCK 2

Cast on 42 sts.
Work 10 rows in k1, p1, rib.
Row 1: *P2, k2 tog, m1, k2, repeat from * to end of row.
Row 2: *P2, k4, repeat from * to end of row.
Row 3: *P2, k2, m1, k2 tog, tbl, repeat from * to end of row.
Row 4: *P2, k4, repeat from * to end of row.
Repeat Rows 1–4 until length desired.
Shape heel thus:
Row 1: K12, turn, sl 1, purlwise, purl to end of row.
Row 2: K11, turn, sl 1, purlwise, purl to end of row.
Continue decreasing in this manner until you have worked k6, turn, sl 1, purlwise, purl to end of row.
Reverse shaping:
K6, pick up loop from row below, knit it with the next st on L.H. needle, turn, sl 1, purlwise, purl to end of row.
Continue knitting 1 extra st with loop until all 12 sts are on needle.
Work 18 sts in pattern, k12.
Work other side of heel thus:
Row 1: P12, turn, sl 1, knit to end of row.
Row 2: P11, turn, sl 1, knit to end of row.
Continue decreasing this way until you have worked p6, turn, sl 1, knit to end of row.
Reverse shaping:
P6, pick up loop from row below, purl it tog with next st on L.H. needle, turn, sl.1, purl to end of row.
Continue this way, purling 1 extra st with loop until all 12 sts are on needle.
Work 18 sts in pattern as Row 2, p12, keeping first and last 12 sts in st st for heel, and centre 18 sts in the 4-row pattern.
Work 3 complete patterns, then shape toe:
Row 1: *K5, k2 tog, repeat from * to end of row.
Row 2 and every alternate row: Purl.
Row 3: *K4, k2 tog, repeat from * to end of row.
Row 4: Purl.
Continue decreasing until 12 sts remain. Break off yarn, thread through sts, fasten off. Sew up sock seam.

SOCK 3

Cast on 34 sts.
Work 6 rows in k1, p1, rib, decreasing 4 sts evenly on row 6 (30 sts).

Pattern:
Row 1: K1, *m1, k2 tog, repeat from * to last st, k1.
Row 2: Purl.
Row 3: K2, *m1, k2 tog, repeat from * to end of row.
Row 4: Purl.
Repeat Rows 1–4 until length desired.
Shape heel thus:
Row 1: †K10, turn, sl 1, purlwise, p to end of row.
Row 2: K9, turn, sl 1, purlwise, p to end of row.
Decrease until you have worked k5, turn, sl 1, purlwise, p to end of row.
Reverse shaping:
K5, pick up loop from row below, knit together with next st on L.H. needle, turn, sl 1, purlwise, purl to end of row.
Continue knitting 1 extra st with loop until all 10 sts are on needle † Knit across all sts (30 sts).
(†–† *is a special reference for next pattern.*)
Other side of heel:
††*Row 1:* P10, turn, sl 1, knit to end of row.
Row 2: P9, turn, sl 1, knit to end of row.
Decrease as above until you have worked p5, turn, sl 1, knit to end of row.
Reverse shaping:
P5, pick up loop from row below, purl it together with next st on L.H. needle, turn, sl 1, k to end of row.
Continue purling 1 extra st with loop until all 10 sts are on needle.
Work 8 rows st st.
Shape toe:
Row 1: *K4, k2 tog, repeat from * to end of row.
Row 2: Purl.
Row 3: *K3, k2 tog, repeat from * to end of row.
Row 4: Purl.
Decrease until you have worked *k1, k2 tog. Repeat from * to end of row (10 sts).
Break off yarn, thread through sts, draw up tightly. Sew up foot and leg seams ††
(††–†† *is a special reference for next pattern.*)

SOCK 4

Cast on 34 sts.
Work 6 rows in k1, p1 rib, decreasing 3 sts evenly on 6th row (31 sts).
Pattern:
Row 1: K1, *m1, sl 1, k1, psso, repeat from * to end of row.
Row 2: P1, *m1, p2 tog, repeat from * to end of row.
Repeat Rows 1–2 12 times or to length desired.
Shape heel:
Follow instructions on Sock 3 from † to † then knit across all sts, decreasing 1 st in this row (30 sts). Work other side of heel as Sock 3 from †† to ††.

Doll Stand Covers

Lilly requires 2 × 20 g balls of DMC 20 Cotton, a pair of 2.75 (12) needles, and a length of ribbon to tie the cover into place.

Annie: One × 50 g ball of 4-ply Cotton, 2.75 (12) needles. Sufficient ribbon or cord to tie four bows to keep stand cover in position.

LILLY

Cast on 27 sts.

Row 1: K24, m2, k2 tog, k1.

Row 2: M1, k2 tog (k 1st loop, drop 2nd loop of m2 of previous row), k23, turn, leaving 1 st on needle.

N.B.: *K 1st loop, drop 2nd loop of m2 of previous row. Always drop the 2nd loop in this particular place. The cotton was turned twice (m2) to make the edge easy and not to form an additional st.*

Row 3: K24, m2, k2.

Row 4: M1, k2 tog, k24, turn, leaving 2 sts on needle.

Row 5: K24, m2, k2.

Row 6: M1, k2 tog, k24, turn, leaving 3 sts on needle.

Row 7: K18, k2 tog, m2, k2 tog, k2, m2, k2.

Row 8: M1, k2 tog, k5, purl 2nd loop of m2 of previous row, k18, turn, leaving 4 sts on needle.

Row 9: K15, k2 tog, m2, (k2 tog) twice, m2, k2 tog, k1, m2, k2.

Row 10: M1, k2 tog, k4, p1, k3, p1, k15, turn, leaving 5 sts on needle.

Row 11: K16, k2 tog, m2, k2 tog, k4, m2, k2.

Row 12: M1, k2 tog, k7, p1, k16, turn, leaving 6 sts on needle.

Row 13: K13, k2 tog, m2, (k2 tog) twice, m2, k2 tog, k3, m2, k2.

Row 14: M1, k2 tog, k6, p1, k3, p1, k13, turn, leaving 7 sts on needle.

Row 15: K14, k2 tog, m2, k2 tog, k6, m2, k2.

Row 16: M1, k2 tog, k9, p1, k14, turn, leaving 8 sts on needle.

Row 17: K8, k2 tog, m2, k2 tog, k6, k2 tog, m2, k2 tog, k2, m1, k2.

Row 18: M1, k2 tog, k5, p1, k9, p1, k8, turn, leaving 9 sts on needle.

Row 19: K5, k2 tog, m2, (k2 tog) twice, m2, k2 tog, k2, k2 tog, m2, (k2 tog) twice, m2, k2 tog, k1, m2, k2.

Row 20: M1, k2 tog, k4, p1, k3, p1, k5, p1, k3, p1, k5, turn, leaving 10 sts on needle.

Row 21: K6, k2 tog, m2, k2 tog, k6, k2 tog, m2, k2 tog, k4, m2, k2.

Row 22: M1, k2 tog, k7, p1, k9, p1, k6, turn, leaving 11 sts on needle.

Row 23: K3, k2 tog, m2, (k2 tog) twice, m2, k2 tog, k2, k2 tog, m2, (k2 tog) twice, m2, (k2 tog) twice, m2, k2 tog, k1.

Row 24: M1, k2 tog, k4, p1, k3, p1, k5, (p1, k3) twice, turn, leaving 12 sts on needle.

Row 25: K4, k2 tog, m2, k2 tog, k6, k2 tog, m2, k2 tog, k1, k2 tog, m2, k2 tog, k1.

Row 26: M1, k2 tog, k5, p1, k9, p1, k4, turn, leaving 13 sts on needle.

Row 27: K8, k2 tog, m2, k2 tog, k5, k2 tog, m2, k2 tog, k1.

Row 28: M1, k2 tog, k9, p1, k8, turn, leaving 14 sts on needle.

Row 29: K5, k2 tog, m2, (k2 tog) twice, m2, k2 tog, k2, k2 tog, m2, k2 tog, k1.

Row 30: M1, k2 tog, k6, p1, k3, p1, k5, turn, leaving 15 sts on needle.

Row 31: K6, k2 tog, m2, k2 tog, k3, k2 tog, m2, k2 tog, k1.

Row 32: M1, k2 tog, k7, p1, k6, turn, leaving 16 sts on needle.

Row 33: K3, k2 tog, m2, (k2 tog) twice, m2, (k2 tog) twice, m2, k2 tog, k1.

Row 34: M1, k2 tog, k4, (p1, k3) twice, turn, leaving 17 sts on needle.

Row 35: K4, k2 tog, m2, k2 tog, k1, k2 tog, m2, k2 tog, k1.

Row 36: M1, k2 tog, k5, p1, k4, turn, leaving 18 sts on needle.

Row 37: K7, k2 tog, m2, k2 tog, k1.

Row 38: M1, k2 tog, k8, turn, leaving 19 sts on needle.

Row 39: K5, k2 tog, m2, k2 tog, k1.

Row 40: M1, k2 tog, k6, turn, leaving 20 sts on needle.

Row 41: K3, k2 tog, m2, k2 tog, k1.

Row 42: M1, k2 tog, k5, (m1, k2 tog) 10 times (27 sts).

Repeat Rows 1–42 until size required. Cast off.

ANNIE

Cast on 35 sts.

Row 1: Sl 1, k23, k2 tog, m1, k4, m1, p2 tog, k1, m1, k2.

Row 2: K4, m1, p2 tog, k28, turn, leaving 2 sts on needle.

Row 3: Sl 1, k20, k2 tog, m1, k5, m1, p2 tog, k2, m1, k2.

Row 4: K5, m1, p2 tog, k26, turn, leaving 4 sts on needle.

Row 5: Sl 1, k17, k2 tog, m1, k6, m1, p2 tog, k3, m1, k2.

Row 6: K6, m1, p2 tog, k24, turn, leaving 6 sts on needle.

Row 7: Sl 1, k14, k2 tog, m1, k7, m1, p2 tog, k2 tog, m1, k2 tog, m1, k2.

Row 8: K5, p1, m1, p2 tog, k22, turn, leaving 8 sts on needle.

Row 9: Sl 1, k11, k2 tog, m1, k1, k2 tog, m1, k1, m1, k2 tog, k2, m1, p2 tog, k6.

Row 10: Cast off 4 sts, k1, m1, p2 tog, k20, turn, leaving 10 sts on needle.

Row 11: Sl 1, k8, k2 tog, m1, k1, k2 tog, m1, k3, m1, k2 tog, k1, m1, p2 tog, m1, k2.

Row 12: K3, m1, p2 tog, k18, turn, leaving 12 sts on needle.

Row 13: Sl 1, k5, k2 tog, m1, k2, k2 tog, m1, k3, m1, k2 tog, k1, m1, p2 tog, k1, m1, k2.

Row 14: K4, m1, p2 tog, k16, turn, leaving 14 sts on needle.

Row 15: Sl 1, k5, m1, k2 tog, k2, m1, k3 tog, m1, k3, m1, p2 tog, k2, m1, k2.

Row 16: K5, m1, p2 tog, k14, turn, leaving 16 sts on needle.

Row 17: Sl 1, k4, m1, k2 tog, k7, m1, p2 tog, k2 tog, m2, k1, m1, k2.

Row 18: K5, p1, k1, m1, p2 tog, k12, turn, leaving 18 sts on needle.

Row 19: Sl 1, k3, m1, k2 tog, k6, m1, p2 tog, k7.

Row 20: Cast off 4 sts, k2, m1, p2 tog, k10, turn, leaving 20 sts on needle.

Row 21: Sl 1, k2, m1, k2 tog, k5, m1, p2 tog, k1, m1, k2.

Row 22: K4, m1, p2 tog, k8, turn, leaving 22 sts on needle.

Row 23: Sl 1, k1, m1, k2 tog, k4, m1, p2 tog, k2, m1, k2.

Row 24: K5, m1, p2 tog, k6, turn, leaving 24 sts on needle.

Row 25: Sl 1, m1, k2 tog, k3, m1, p2 tog, k3, m1, k2.

Row 26: K6, m1, p2 tog, k4, turn, leaving 26 sts on needle.

Row 27: Sl 1, k3, m1, p2 tog, k2 tog, m2, k2 tog, m1, k2.

Row 28: K5, p1, k1, m1, p2 tog, k2, turn, leaving 28 sts on needle.

Row 29: Sl 1, k1, m1, p2 tog, k7.

Row 30: Cast off 4 sts, k2, m1, p2 tog, k30.

Repeat Rows 1–30 until work forms a circle.

Cast off.

Work a row of crochet along both ends of cover to thread ribbon or cord ties through.

Circular Tablecloth: LOMAS LACE

An exquisite piece of knitting.
The circular tablecloth has a diameter of 30'' (76 cm). Knitted on 2.75 needles using 6 balls of 3-ply
cotton. Make a circular lining to match or contrast with the lace. Lomas lace is knitted on two needles.
Tablecloth by Edna Lomas.

Cast on 8 sts.

Row 1: Inc in each st (16 sts).

Row 2: As Row 1 (32 sts).

Row 3: *P2, m2, p2, repeat from * to end of row.

Row 4: *P1, p2 tog, m2, p2 tog, p1, repeat from * to end of row.

Rows 5 and 6: As Row 4 (48 sts).

Row 7: *P1, pick up thread before next st, p2 tog, m2, p2 tog, pick up thread, p1, repeat from * to end of row (64 sts).

Row 8: *P2, p2 tog, m2, p2 tog, p2, repeat from * to end of row.

Rows 9 and 10: As Row 8.

Row 11: *P1, pick up thread, p1, p2 tog, m2, p2 tog, p1, pick up thread, p1, repeat from * to end of row (80 sts).

Row 12: *P3, p2 tog, m2, p2 tog, p3, repeat from * to end of row.

Rows 13 and 14: As Row 12.

Row 15: *P1, pick up thread, p2, p2 tog, m2, p2 tog, p2, pick up thread, p1, repeat from * to end of row.

Row 16: *P4, p2 tog, m2, p2 tog, p4, repeat from * to end of row.

Rows 17 and 18: As Row 16.

Row 19: *P1, pick up thread, p3, p2 tog, m2, p2 tog, p3, pick up thread, p1, repeat from * to end of row.

Row 20: *P5, p2 tog, m2, p2 tog, p5, repeat from * to end of row.

Rows 21 and 22: As Row 20.

Continue inc on every 4th row until you have worked *P1, pick up thread, p17, p2 tog, m2, p2 tog, p17, pick up thread, p1, repeat from * to end of row (336 sts). Continue thus, working lace pattern.

Row 1: *P19, p2 tog, m1, p2 tog, p19, repeat from * to end of row.

Row 2: *P18, p2 tog, m1, p1, m1, p2 tog, p18, repeat from * to end of row.

Row 3: *P17, p2 tog, m1, p3, m1, p2 tog, p17, repeat from * to end of row.

Row 4: *P16, p2 tog, m1, p1, m1, p3 tog, m1, p1, m1, p2 tog, p16, repeat from * to end of row.

Row 5: *P15, p2 tog, m1, p3, m1, p1, m1, p3, m1, p2 tog, p15, repeat from * to end of row.

Row 6: *P14, p2 tog, m1, p1, m1, p3 tog, m1, p3, m1, p3 tog, m1, p1, m1, p2 tog, p14, repeat from * to end of row.

Row 7: *P13, p2 tog, m1, p3, m1, p1, m1, p2 tog, p1, p2 tog, m1, p1, m1, p3, m1, p2 tog, p13, repeat from * to end of row.

Row 8: *P12, p2 tog, m1, p1, m1, p3 tog, m1, (p3, m1, p3 tog, m1) twice, p1, m1, p2 tog, p12, repeat from * to end of row.

Row 9: *P11, p2 tog, m1, p3, m1, p1, m1, (p2 tog, p1, p2 tog, m1, p1, m1) twice, p3, m1, p2 tog, p11, repeat from * to end of row.

Row 10: *P10, p2 tog, m1, p1, (m1, p3 tog, m1, p3) 3 times, m1, p3 tog, m1, p1, m1, p2 tog, p10, repeat from * to end of row.

Row 11: *P9, p2 tog, m1, p3, (m1, p1, m1, p2 tog, p1, p2 tog) 3 times, m1, p1, m1, p3, m1, p2 tog, p9, repeat from * to end of row.

Row 12: *P8, p2 tog, m1, p1, (m1, p3 tog, m1, p3) 4 times, m1, p1, m1, p2 tog, p8, repeat from * to end of row.

Row 13: *P7, p2 tog, m1, p3, m1, p1, (m1, p2 tog, p1, p2 tog, m1, p1) 4 times, m1, p3, m1, p2 tog, p7, repeat from * to end of row.

Row 14: *P6, p2 tog, m1, p1, (m1, p3 tog, m1, p3) 6 times, m1, p3 tog, m1, p1, m1, p2 tog, p6, repeat from * to end of row.

Row 15: *P5, p2 tog, m1, p3, (m1, p1, m1, p2 tog, p1, p2 tog) 5 times, m1, p1, m1, p3, m1, p2 tog, p5, repeat from * to end of row.

Row 16: *P4, p2 tog, m1, p1, (m1, p3 tog, m1, p3) 6 times, m1, p3 tog, m1, p1, m1, p2 tog, p4, repeat from * to end of row.

Row 17: *P3, p2 tog, m1, p3, (m1, p1, m1, p2 tog, p1, p2 tog) 6 times, m1, p1, m1, p3, m1, p2 tog, p3, repeat from * to end of row.

Row 18: *P2, p2 tog, m1, p1, (m1, p3 tog, m1, p3) 7 times, m1, p3 tog, m1, p1, m1, p2 tog, p2, repeat from * to end of row.

Row 19: *P1, p2 tog, m1, p3, (m1, p1, m1, p2 tog, p1, p2 tog) 7 times, m1, p1, m1, p3, m1, p2 tog, p1, repeat from * to end of row.

Row 20: *P2 tog, m1, p1 (m1, p3 tog, m1, p3) 8 times, m1, p3 tog, m1, p1, m1, p2 tog, repeat from * to end of row.

Row 21: P1, *m1, p3, (m1, p1, m1, p2 tog, p1, p2 tog) 8 times, m1, p1, m1, p3, m1, p2 tog, repeat from * to last st, p1.

Row 22: *P2, m1, p3 tog, m1, p1, repeat from * to last st, p1.

Row 23: *P1, p2 tog, m1, p1, m1, p2 tog, repeat from * to last st, p1.

Row 24: P2 tog, *m1, p3, m1, p3 tog, repeat from * to last 5 sts, m1, p3, m1, p2 tog.

Row 25: *P1, m1, p2 tog, p1, p2 tog, m1, repeat from * to last st, p1.

Change to next size needle (the larger needle will make the cloth hang better).

Continue repeating last 4 rows until work measures approx. 16'' (41 cm) from centre. Change to larger needle. Repeat last 4 rows for approx. 2'' (5 cm).

Lace edging

Cast on 11 sts at end of last row.

Edging is worked on these sts, working off all sts of cloth

until 11 sts remain.

Row 1: M1, p3 tog, (m1, p2 tog) 4 times, m1, p1, p2 tog.

Row 2: P2 tog, (m1, p2 tog) 4 times, m1, p1, p2 tog.

Row 3: (M1, p2 tog) 5 times, m1, p1, p2 tog.

Row 4: P2 tog, p1, (m1, p2 tog) 4 times, m1, p2.

Row 5: (M1, p2 tog) 5 times, m1, p2, p2 tog.

Row 6: P2 tog, p2, (m1, p2 tog) 4 times, m1, p2.

Row 7: (M1, p2 tog) 5 times, m1, p3, p2 tog.

Row 8: P2 tog, p3, (m1, p2 tog) 4 times, m1, p2.

Row 9: (M1, p2 tog) 5 times, m1, p4, p2 tog.

Row 10: P2 tog, p4, (m1, p2 tog) 4 times, m1, p2.

Row 11: (M1, p2 tog) 5 times, m1, p5, p2 tog.

Row 12: P2 tog, p5, (m1, p2 tog) 4 times, m1, p2.

Row 13: M1, p3 tog, (m1, p2 tog) 4 times, m1, p5, p2 tog.

Row 14: P2 tog, p4, (m1, p2 tog) 5 times, p1.

Row 15: M1, p3 tog, (m1, p2 tog) 4 times, m1, p4, p2 tog.

Row 16: P2 tog, p3, (m1, p2 tog) 5 times, p1.

Row 17: M1, p3 tog, (m1, p2 tog) 4 times, m1, p3, p2 tog.

Row 18: P2 tog, p2, (m1, p2 tog) 5 times, p1.

Row 19: M1, p3 tog, (m1, p2 tog) 4 times, m1, p2, p2 tog.

Row 20: P2 tog, p1, (m1, p2 tog) 5 times, p1.

Repeat Rows 1–20 until edging of tablecloth is completed, and you have 11 sts on needle. Cast off. Sew cloth from centre to lace edge. Gently press work, and form circle.

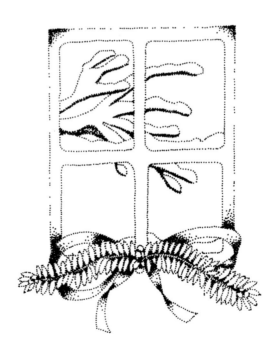

Three Doilies

Three delightful doilies, each approximately 4½ '' (11 cm) in diameter. Each requires 1 × 20 g ball of DMC 20 Cotton. Knitted on a set of 2 mm (14) needles.

SHEENA

Approx. 4½ '' (11 cm) diameter
Using DMC 20 Cotton and set of 4 needles, cast on 8 sts. Arrange on 3 needles 2-2-4 sts. Work with 4th needle.

Round 1: Knit.
Round 2 and even numbered rounds: Knit (k1, p1, in m2, of previous round where applicable).
Round 3: K1, tbl, m2, k1, tbl, m2 to end of round.
Round 5: K1, tbl, m1, k2, m1, k1, tbl, m1, k2, m1, repeat to end of round.
Round 7: K1, tbl, m1, sl 1, k1, psso, k2, m1, k1, tbl, m1, k2, k2 tog, m1, repeat to end of round.
Round 9: K1, tbl, m1, sl 1, k1, psso, k3, m1, k1, tbl, m1, k3, k2 tog, m1, repeat to end of round.
Round 11: K1, tbl, m1, sl 1, k1, psso, k4, m1, k1, tbl, m1, k4, k2 tog, m1, repeat to end of round.
Round 13: K1, tbl, m1, k2, k2 tog, m1, k7, m1, sl 1, k1, psso, k2, m1, repeat to end of round.
Round 15: K1, tbl, m1, k2, k2 tog, m1, k9, m1, sl 1, k1, psso, k2, m1, repeat to end of round.
Round 17: K3, k2 tog, m1, k1, tbl, m1, sl 1, k1, psso, k5, k2 tog, m1, k1, tbl, m1, sl 1, k1, psso, k2, repeat to end of round.
Round 19: K2, k2 tog, m1, k2 tog, m1, k1, tbl, m1, sl 1, k1, psso, k3, k2 tog, m1, k1, tbl, m1, sl 1, k1, psso, m1, sl 1, k1, psso, k1, repeat to end of round.
Round 21: K1, k2 tog, (m1, k2 tog) twice, m1, k1, tbl, m1, sl 1, k1, psso, k1, k2 tog, m1, k1, tbl, m1, sl 1, k1, psso, m1, sl 1, k1, psso, m1, sl 1, k1, psso, repeat to end of round.
Round 23: Move 1 st from R.H. needle to L.H. needle, sl 1, k2 tog, psso, (m1, k2 tog) 3 times, m1, k1, tbl, m1, sl 1, k2 tog, psso, m1, tbl, (m1, sl 1, k1, psso) 3 times, m1, repeat to end of round.
Round 24: Move 1 st from R.H. needle to L.H. needle. Using 0.75 crochet hook, work *dc into next 3 sts, slip off, 5 ch, dc into next 2 sts, slip off, 5 ch, repeat from * ending with slip st into 1st dc. Fasten off.

TONI

Approx. 4¾ '' (12 cm) diameter
Cast on 10 sts. Arrange on 3 needles 2-3-5 sts. Work with 4th needle.
Rounds 1-5: Knit.
Round 6: K1, m1, repeat to end of round.
Round 7 and alternate rounds: Knit.
Round 8: K1, m1, repeat to end of round.
Round 10: K1, m1, k3, m1, repeat to end of round.
Round 12: K1, m1, k1, k3 tog, k1, m1, repeat to end of round.
Round 14: K2, m1, k3 tog, m1, k1, repeat to end of round.

Round 16: K3, m1, k1, m1, k2, repeat to end of round.
Round 18: Move 1 st from R.H. needle to L.H. needle, k3 tog, k2, m1, k1, m1, k2, repeat to end of round.
Round 20: Move 1 st from R.H. needle to L.H. needle, k1, m1, k3, m1, k1, repeat to end of round.
Round 22: Move 1 st from R.H. needle to L.H. needle, k3 tog, m1, k5, m1, repeat to end of round.
Round 24: K1, m1, k2, k3 tog, k2, m1, repeat to end of round.
Round 26: K2, m1, k2, k3 tog, k1, m1, k1, repeat to end of round.
Round 28: K3, m1, k3 tog, m1, k2, repeat to end of round.
Round 30: K4, m1, k1, m1, k3, repeat to end of round.
Round 32: Move 1 st from R.H. needle to L.H. needle, knit to end of round.
Using 0.75 crochet hook *dc into next 3 sts, slip off. 5 ch dc into next 2 sts, slip off, 5 ch. Repeat from * ending with sl st into 1st dc. Fasten off.

ALISON

Approx. 4¾ '' (12 cm) diameter
Cast on 16 sts. Arrange on 3 needles 4-4-8 sts.
Rounds 1,2,3: Knit.
Round 4: K1, m1, k1, repeat to end of round.
Round 5 and all odd numbered rounds: Knit.
Round 6: K1, m1, k1, tbl, m1, k1, repeat to end of round.
Round 8: K2, m1, k1, tbl, m1, k1, repeat to end of round.
Round 10: M1, k7, repeat to end of round.
Round 12: M1, k1, tbl, m1, sl 1, k1, psso, k3, k2 tog, repeat to end of round.
Round 14: K1, m1, k1, tbl, m1, k1, sl 1, k1, psso, k1, k2 tog, repeat to end of round.
Round 16: K2, m1, k1, tbl, m1, k2, m1, sl 1, k2 tog, psso, m1, repeat to end of round.
Round 18: K7, m1, k3, m1, repeat to end of round.
Round 20: Sl 1, k1, psso, k3, k2 tog, m1, k2 tog, m1, k1, m1, sl 1, k1, psso, m1, repeat to end of round.
Round 22: Sl 1, k1, psso, k1, k2 tog, m1, k2 tog, m1, k3, m1, sl 1, k1, psso, m1, repeat to end of round.
Round 24: Sl 1, k2 tog, psso, (m1, k2 tog) twice, m1, k1, m1, sl 1, k1, psso, m1, sl 1, k1, psso, m1, repeat to end of round.
Round 26: K1, k2 tog, m1, k2 tog, (m1, k1) 3 times, (m1, sl 1, k1, psso) twice, repeat to end of round.
Round 28: (M1, k2 tog) twice, k1, m1, k1, tbl, m1, k1, sl 1, k1, psso, m1, sl 1, k1, psso, sl 1, k2 tog, psso, repeat to end of round.
Round 29: Knit.
Slip 1 st from L.H. needle to R.H. needle. With 0.75 crochet hook work *dc into 3 sts, slip off, 5 ch. Repeat from * ending with a slip st into 1st dc. Fasten off.

Flower and Leaf Trims

Knit yourself a flower, or a leaf!
These attractive trims can be used to decorate a doll's hat or other garment. The trims illustrated were knitted in DMC 20 Cotton on 2 mm (14) needles. The quantity of thread will depend on your choice of yarn and needles.

The three large flowers are 'Judith Mansfield'; a string of small flowers appears on the left; three open flowers appear at the bottom, while a spray of oval leaves is attached to a large triangular leaf on the right.

FLOWER 'JUDITH MANSFIELD'

Worked in layers. Cast on 2 sts.

Layer 1

Row 1: M1, knit to end.
Row 2: Sl 1, k to end.
Repeat Rows 1 and 2 until there are 9 sts on needle, ending with row 2.
Row 3: M1, k3 tog, k to end.
Row 4: Sl 1, k to end.
Repeat from Row 1 until 9 petals have been worked. Cast off.

Layer 2

Work as 1st layer until petal has 7 sts. Decrease until 2 sts remain.
Make 9 petals. Cast off.

Layer 3

Work as 1st layer until petal has 5 sts. Make 5 petals. Cast off.
Thread yarn through straight edges, draw up to form circles. Stitch layers together to form flower.

SMALL FLOWER

Cast on 10 sts.
Row 1: K1, *m1, k1*, repeat *-* to end.
Repeat Row 1 twice. Cast off.

OPEN FLOWER

Cast on 4 sts.
Row 1: M1, k2 tog, k2.
Repeat Row 1 29 times.
Cast off, leaving long thread. With coarse needle pick up the loops along edge of work, draw up to form open flower, stitch into position.

OVAL LEAF

Cast on 3 sts.
Row 1: K1, (m1, k1) twice.
Row 2 and alternate rows: Purl.
Row 3: K2, m1, k1, m1, k2.
Row 5: K3, m1, k1, m1, k3.
Row 7: K4, m1, k1, m1, k4.

Row 9: Knit.
Row 11: K4, sl 1, k2 tog, psso, k4.
Row 13: K3, sl 1, k2 tog, psso, k3.
Row 15: K2, sl 1, k2 tog, psso, k2.
Row 17: K1, sl 1, k2 tog, psso, k1.
Row 19: Sl 1, k2 tog, psso.
Cast off.

LARGE TRIANGULAR LEAF

Cast on 24 sts.
Row 1: Knit.
Row 2: K1, sl 1, k1, psso, knit to last 3 sts, k2 tog, k1.
Rows 3, 4 & 5: Knit.
Repeat from Row 2 until 6 sts remain, ending pattern with Row 5. On next row, k1, sl 1, psso, k2 tog, k1, on remaining sts (k2 tog) twice.
Last row, knit remaining 2 sts together.
Cast off.
Using yarn needle, thread through cast-on stitches, draw into leaf base. With 4 leaves worked, and threading yarn through the 4 bases, a circle of leaves will be formed to frame a flower.

Braids

Five useful braids to use in various ways, all knitted on 2 mm (14) needles using DMC 20 Cotton. Shown from left to right are coral, bobble, gimp, cord and ruffles braids.

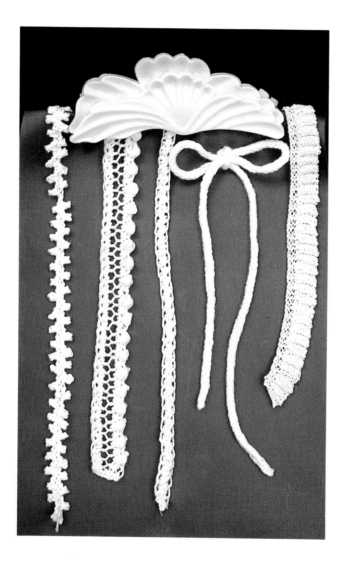

BOBBLE

Cast on 6 sts.
Rows 1, 2 & 3: Sl 1, purlwise, k2, m1, k2 tog, k1.
Row 4: Work 6 sts in 1 st st (by knitting in f & b of st 3 times), sl the 5th st over the 6th st, k2, m1, k2 tog, k1.
Repeat Rows 1–4 until length desired. Cast off.

GIMP

Cast on 3 sts.
Row 1: M1, k2 tog, k1.
Row 2: K3.
Repeat Rows 1–2 until length desired.

CORD

Using dpn cast on 3 sts.
Row 1: *K3, do not turn. Slide sts to other side of needle*. Repeat *–* until length desired. Cast off.

RUFFLES

Cast on 9 sts.
Row 1: Knit.
Row 2: P7, turn.
Row 3: K7.
Row 4: P7, k2.
Row 5: K2, p7.
Row 6: K7, turn.
Row 7: P7.
Row 8: Knit.
Repeat Rows 1–8 until length desired. Cast off.

CORAL

Cast on 4 sts.
Row 1: Cast off 2 sts, k1.
Row 2: Cast on 2 sts, k and cast off the 2 sts, k1.
Repeat Row 2 until length desired. Cast off.

Beadings

These beadings, knitted in fine thread, are ideal to trim your dolls' underwear. The small number of stitches required make ideal knitting while watching television or travelling.
The beadings are numbered 1 to 6 from left to right.

BEADING 1

Cast on 6 sts.
Row 1: Sl 1, k2 tog, m2, k2 tog, k1.
Row 2: Sl 1, k2, p1, k2.
Row 3: Knit.
Row 4: Knit.
Repeat Rows 1–4 until length desired. Cast off.

BEADING 2

Cast on 5 sts.
Row 1: K2 tog, m2, k2 tog, k1.
Row 2: Sl 1, k2, p1, k1.
Repeat Rows 1–2 until length desired. Cast off.

BEADING 3

Cast on 8 sts.
Row 1: K2 tog, m2, k2 tog, k1, m2, k2 tog, k1.
Row 2: Sl 1, k2, p1, k2 tog, k1, p1, k1.
Repeat Rows 1–2 until length desired. Cast off.

BEADING 4

Cast on 8 sts.
Row 1: Knit.
Row 2: M1, k2 tog, k6.
Row 3: M1, k2 tog, cast off 4 sts, k1.
Row 4: M1, k2 tog, turn, cast on 4 sts, turn, k2.
Row 5: As Row 2.
Repeat Rows 2–5 until length desired. Cast off.

BEADING 5

Cast on 8 sts.
Row 1: M1, k2 tog, k6.
Row 2: M1, k2 tog, k1, k2 tog, m2, k2 tog, k1.
Row 3: M1, k2 tog, k1, p1, k4.
Repeat Rows 1–3 until length desired. Cast off.

BEADING 6

Cast on 6 sts.
Row 1: Sl 1, k2, m1, k2 tog, k1.
Repeat Row 1 until length desired. Cast off.

Edgings

Six delicate lace edgings. Use the yarn and needles of your choice.

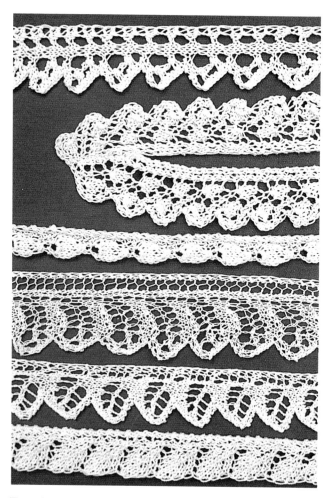

Top to bottom: eyelet edging, mitred edging, harebell lace, sea-spray edging, foliage lace and wreath of leaves.

Four beautiful samples of lace knitting. Suitable for trimming the finest fabrics. An excellent way of using left-over yarn.

Top to bottom: Launceston lace, antique lace, fan lace and catkin lace.

EYELET EDGING

Cast on 8 sts.
Row 1: Sl 1, k2 tog, m2, k2 tog, k1, m4, k2.
Row 2: K2, work 4 sts in m4 of previous row, k3, p1, k2.
Row 3: Sl 1, k11.
Row 4: K12.
Row 5: Sl 1, k2 tog, m2, k2 tog, k1, *m2, k2 tog, repeat from * twice.
Row 6: *K2, p1, repeat from * twice, k3, p1, k2.
Row 7: Sl 1, k14.
Row 8: Cast off 7 sts, k7.
Repeat Rows 1–8 until length desired. Cast off.

MITRED EDGING

Work begins on point of corner.
Cast on 6 sts, purl one row.
Row 1: Cast on 1 st and knit it, k1, (m1, k1) 3 times, m1, k2.
Row 2: P11.
Row 3: Cast on 1 st and knit it, k2 tog, m1, k3, m1, k1, m1, k3, m1, k2.
Row 4: P15.
Row 5: Cast on 1 st and knit it. M1, k2 tog, *m1, sl 1, (k2 tog) twice, pss and 1st k2 tog over 2nd k2 tog, m1, k1, repeat from *, k1.
Row 6: Cast off 4 sts, p7, inc in last st by p and k in same st.
This finishes slope of mitre.

Straight pattern begins:
Row 1: Sl 1, k1, m1, k2 tog, (m1, k1) 3 times, m1, k2.
Row 2: P13.
Row 3: Sl 1, k1, m1, k2 tog, m1, k3, m1, k1, m1, k3, m1, k2.
Row 4: P17.
Row 5: Sl 1, k1, m1, k2 tog, *m1, sl 1, (k2 tog) twice, pss and 1st k2 tog over 2nd k2 tog, m1, k1, repeat from *, k1.
Row 6: Cast off 4 sts, p5.
Row 7: Sl 1, k1, psso, (m1, k1) twice, m1, k2.
Row 8: P8.
Row 9: Sl 1, k1, psso, m1, k1, m1, k3, m1, k2.
Row 10: P10.
Row 11: Sl 1, k1, psso, k1, sl 1, (k2 tog) twice, pss and 1st k2 tog over 2nd k2 tog, k2.
Row 12: Cast off 5 sts.
Repeat straight lace Rows 1–12 until length desired. Sew mitred corners together on wrong side of work.

HAREBELL LACE

Cast on 6 sts.
Row 1: P1, (k1, p1, k1, p1, k1) in next st, p2, m1, p2 tog.
Row 2: K4, p5, k1.
Row 3: P1, k5, p2, m1, p2 tog.
Row 4: K4, p5, k1.
Row 5: P1, sl 1, k1, psso, k1, k2 tog.
Row 6: K4, p3, k1.
Row 7: P1, sl 1, k2 tog, psso, p2, m1, p2 tog.
Row 8: K4, p2.
Repeat Rows 1–8 until length desired. Cast off.

SEA-SPRAY EDGING

Cast on 17 sts.
Row 1: Sl 1, k2, m1, k2 tog, (k1, m1) 3 times, k4, (m2, k2 tog) twice, k1.
Row 2: K3, p1, k2, p1, k12, m1, k2 tog, k1.
Row 3: Sl 1, k2, m1, (k2 tog) twice, m1, k2, m1, k1, m1, sl 1, k2 tog, psso, k9.
Row 4: K19, m1, k2 tog, k1.
Row 5: Sl 1, k2, m1, (k2 tog) twice, m1, k3, m1, k1, m1, sl 1, k2 tog, psso, k3, (m2, k2 tog) twice, k1.
Row 6: K3, p1, k2, p1, k14, m1, k2 tog, k1.
Row 7: Sl 1, k2, m1, (k2 tog) twice, m1, k4, m1, k1, m1, sl 1, k2 tog, psso, k9.
Row 8: Cast off 7 sts, k13, m1, k2 tog, k1.
Repeat Rows 1–8 until length desired. Cast off.

FOLIAGE LACE

Cast on 9 sts.
Row 1: K2, m1, (k2 tog, m2) twice, k2 tog, k1.
Row 2: K3, p1, k2, p1, k1, p1, k2.
Row 3: K2, m1, k2 tog, k2, (m2, k2 tog) twice, k1.
Row 4: K3, p1, k2, p1, k3, p1, k2.
Row 5: K3, m1, k2 tog, k3, (m2, k2 tog) twice, k1.
Row 6: K3, p1, k2, p1, k5, p1, k2.
Row 7: K2, m1, k2 tog, k6, (m2, k2 tog) twice, k1.
Row 8: K3, p1, k2, p1, k7, p1, k2.
Row 9: K2, m1, k2 tog, k13.
Row 10: Cast off 8 sts, k5, p1, k2.
Repeat Rows 1–10 until length desired. Cast off.

WREATH OF LEAVES

Cast on 12 sts.
Row 1: M1, k1, m1, k2, (k2 tog) twice, k2, m1, k2 tog, k1.
Row 2: Purl.
Row 3: M1, k3, m1, k1, (k2 tog) twice, k1, m1, k2 tog, k1.
Row 4: Purl.
Row 5: M1, k5, m1, (k2 tog) twice, m1, k2 tog, k1.
Row 6: Purl.
Row 7: M1, k3, k2 tog, k2, (m1, k2 tog) twice, k1.
Row 8: Purl.
Repeat Rows 1–8 until length desired. Cast off.

LAUNCESTON LACE

Cast on 17 sts.
Row 1: Sl 1, k2, k2 tog, m1, k3, k2 tog, m1, k5, m2, k2.
Row 2: K3, p1, k3, k2 tog, m1, k3, k2 tog, m1, k2, m1, k2 tog, k1.
Row 3: Sl 1, k5, m1, k2 tog, k3, m1, k2 tog, k2, m2, k2 tog, m2, k2.
Row 4: K3, p1, k2, p1, k1, k2 tog, m1, k3, k2 tog, m1, k4, m1, k2 tog, k1.
Row 5: Sl 1, k7, m1, k2 tog, k3, m1, k2 tog, k5, k2 tog.
Row 6: K8, m1, k2 tog, k3, m1, k2 tog, k3, m1, k2 tog, k1.
Row 7: Sl 1, k4, k2 tog, m1, k3, k2 tog, m1, k9.
Row 8: Cast off 4 sts, k5, m1, k2 tog, k3, m1, k2 tog, k1, m1, k2 tog, k1.
Repeat Rows 1–8 until length desired. Cast off.

ANTIQUE LACE

Cast on 13 sts.

Knit 1 row.

Row 1: Sl 1, k1, m1, sl 1, k1, psso, m1, k1, m1, sl 1, k2 tog, psso, m1, k3, m1, k2.

Row 2: K4, (k1, p1) 3 times in next st, p2, k1, p3, k4.

Row 3: Sl 1, k1, m1, sl 1, k1, psso, (k1, p1) 3 times in next st, sl 1, k1, psso, p1, k2 tog, cast off 5 sts, k2, m1, k2.

Row 4: K5, m1, (k1, p1) twice, cast off 5 sts, k4.

Row 5: Sl 1, k1, m1, sl 1, k1, psso, m1, k1, m1, sl 1, k2 tog, psso, m1, k3, m1, k2 tog, m1, k2.

Row 6: K6, (k1, p1) 3 times in next st, p2, k1, p3, k4.

Row 7: Sl 1, k1, m1, sl 1, k1, psso, (k1, p1) 3 times in next st, k1, p2, sl 1, k1, psso, p1, k2 tog, cast off 5 sts, k2, m1, k2 tog, m1, k2.

Row 8: Cast off 4 sts, k2, m1, p1, k1, p1, k1, cast off 5 sts, k4.

Repeat Rows 1–8 until length desired. Cast off.

FAN LACE

Cast on 7 sts.

Row 1: K5, m1, k2.

Row 2 and alternate rows: M1, k2 tog, k to end of row.

Row 3: K4, m1, k2 tog, m1, k2.

Row 5: K3, (m1, k2 tog) twice, m1, k2.

Row 7: K2, (m1, k2 tog) 3 times, m1, k2.

Row 9: K2, (k2 tog, m1) 3 times, k2 tog, k1.

Row 11: K3, (k2 tog, m1) twice, k2 tog, k1.

Row 13: K4, k2 tog, m1, k2 tog, k1.

Row 15: K5, k2 tog, k1.

Row 16: As Row 2.

Repeat Rows 1–16 until length desired. Cast off.

CATKIN LACE

Cast on 8 sts.

Row 1: Sl 1, k1, (m1, k2 tog) twice, k1, m3, k1.

Row 2: K2, p1, k8.

Row 3: Sl 1, k1, m1, k2 tog, k1, m1, k2 tog, k4.

Row 4: K11.

Row 5: Sl 1, k1, m1, k2 tog, k2, m1, k2 tog, k3.

Row 6: Cast off 3 sts, k7.

Repeat Rows 1–6 until length desired. Cast off.

Jarrah Bed

Approximate measurements: 10" × 14" × 20" high (25 cm × 36 cm × 50 cm high).
The bed hangings were knitted on 2 mm (14) needles using DMC Blanc 5200 Size 20 Cotton. The
quantity of cotton will depend on the size of the bed. For the bed illustrated 10 × 20 g balls would be
adequate. The doona edging (Torchon), hangings and tassels should be of the same dye lot. The bedcover is
embroidered in DMC Stranded Cotton. Pillows and bolster are Rose White designs (see page 59).
You will need to make 16 tiny tassels to trim the bed. The bedlinen should be edged with a finer thread
(DMC 100 Blanc 5200).

SPEEDWELL LACE EDGING

Cast on 19 sts.
Row 1: K3, m1, k2 tog, k2, m1, k1, m1, k2 tog, k1, k2 tog, m1, k2, (m2, k2 tog) twice.
Row 2: (K2, p1) twice, k2 tog, k1, m1, sl 1, k2 tog, psso, m1, k3, m1, (k2 tog) twice, m1, k2 tog, k1.
Row 3: K3, (m1, k2 tog) twice, k1, k2 tog, (m1, k1) twice, k2 tog, k6.
Row 4: Cast off 2 sts, k5, m1, k3, m1, sl 1, k2 tog, psso, m1, k3, m1, k2 tog, k1.
Repeat Rows 1–4 until length desired. Cast off.

JARRAH CURTAIN

Cast on multiples of 4, plus 1 st, to make width required.
Row 1: P1, *m1, p3, m1, p1, repeat from * to end of row.
Row 2: K2, *p3 tog, k3, repeat from * to last 2 sts, k2.
Row 3: P2, *m1, p1, m1, p3, repeat from * to last 2 sts, p2.
Row 4: P2 tog, *k3, p3 tog, repeat from * to last 2 sts, p2 tog.
Repeat Rows 1–4 until length desired. Cast off.

SPEEDWELL, STRAIGHT-EDGED LACE, OR INSERTION

Cast on 21 sts.
Row 1: K3, m1, k2 tog, k2, m1, k1, m1, k2 tog, k1, k2 tog, m1, k1, m1, k4, m1, k2 tog, k1.
Row 2: K3, m1, (k2 tog) twice, m1, k3, m1, sl 1, k2 tog, psso, m1, k3, m1, k2 tog, k2, m1, k2 tog, k1.
Row 3: K3, m1, k3 tog, m1, k2 tog, k1, k2 tog, m1, k1, m1, k2 tog, k1, k2 tog, m1, k2 tog, k1, m1, k2 tog, k1.
Row 4: K3, m1, k2 tog, k1, m1, sl 1, k2 tog, psso, m1, k3, m1, sl 1, k2 tog, psso, m1, k3, m1, k2 tog, k1.
Repeat Rows 1–4 until length desired. Cast off.

TORCHON (DOONA COVER)

Cast on 27 sts.
Row 1: Sl 1, k2, m1, k2 tog, k1, m1, k2 tog, k3, k2 tog, m1, k1, m1, sl 1, k1, psso, k5, k2 tog, m1, k1, m1, k2 tog, k1.
Row 2: K2, p17, k5, m1, k2 tog, k1.
Row 3: Sl 1, k2, m1, k2 tog, k1, m1, k2 tog, k2, k2 tog, m1, k3, m1, sl 1, k1, psso, k3, k2 tog, m1, k3, m1, k2.
Row 4: K2, p18, k5, m1, k2 tog, k1.
Row 5: Sl 1, k2, m1, k2 tog, k1, m1, k2 tog, k1, k2 tog, m1, k2 tog, m1, k1, m1, sl 1, k1, psso, m1, sl 1, k1, psso, k1, k2 tog, m1, k2 tog, m1, k1, m1, sl 1, k1, psso, m1, k2.
Row 6: K2, p19, k5, m1, k2 tog, k1.
Row 7: Sl 1, k2, m1, k2 tog, k1, m1, (k2 tog) twice, m1, k2 tog, m1, k3, m1, sl 1, k1, psso, m1, sl 1, k2 tog, psso, m1, k2 tog, m1, k3, m1, sl 1, k1, psso, m1, k2.
Row 8: K2, p20, k5, m1, k2 tog, k1.
Row 9: Sl 1, k2, m1, k2 tog, k1, m1, k2 tog, k1, m1, k2 tog, m1, sl 1, k1, psso, k1, k2 tog, m1, sl 1, k1, psso, m1, k1, m1, k2 tog, m1, sl 1, k1, psso, k1, k2 tog, m1, sl 1, k1, psso, m1, k2.
Row 10: K2, p20, k5, m1, k2 tog, k1.
Row 11: Sl 1, k2, m1, k2 tog, k1, m1, k2 tog, k2, m1, sl 1, k1, psso, m1, sl 1, k2 tog, psso, m1, k2 tog, m1, k3, m1, sl 1, k1, psso, m1, sl 1, k2 tog, psso, (m1, k2 tog) twice, k1.
Row 12: K2, p19, k5, m1, k2 tog, k1.
Row 13: Sl 1, k2, m1, k2 tog, k1, m1, k2 tog, k3, m1, sl 1, k1, psso, k1, k2 tog, m1, k5, m1, sl 1, k1, psso, k1, k2 tog, m1, k2 tog, k1.
Row 14: K2, p18, k5, m1, k2 tog, k1.

Detail of the coverings on the Jarrah bed.

Row 15: Sl 1, k2, m1, k2 tog, k1, m1, k2 tog, k4, m1, sl 1, k2 tog, psso, m1, k7, m1, sl 1, k2 tog, psso, m1, k2 tog, k1.
Row 16: K2, p17, k5, m1, k2 tog, k1.
Repeat Rows 1–16 until length desired. Cast off.

Cedar Bed

A tiny antique four-poster made from Australian cedar.
Approximate measurements are: 6'' × 12'' × 14'' high (15 cm × 30 cm × 35 cm high).
The bedcover required 5 balls DMC 100 Cotton and was knitted on size 20 needles. The bed hangings:
3 balls DMC 100 Cotton, knitted on size 20 needles. Pillow and pillow edgings used 4 balls DMC 20
Cotton on 1.25 needles. Little flowers were embroidered in the corner of each tiny square, and on the
continental pillow corners, using DMC Stranded Cotton (Shades 819 and 523 for a delicate look).

Above: *Close of up cedar bed, showing details of valance.*
Right: *Close up of cedar bed showing bedspread and continental pillows. The raised leaf squares on the bedcover measure less than 2'' (5 cm).*

ALICE ROSE VALANCE

Cast on 33 sts.

Row 1: Sl 1, k21, m1, k2 tog, k2, k2 tog, m1, k2 tog, m3, k2 tog, inc in last st by knitting b and f of st (referred to as 'inc 1' for rest of pattern).

Row 2: K4, p1, k7, p19, turn, leaving 4 sts on needle.

Row 3: Sl 1, k18, m1, k2 tog, k2, k2 tog, k6.

Row 4: Cast off 3 sts, k6, p20, k4.

Row 5: Sl 1, k5, *m1, k2 tog*, repeat *-* 6 times, k4, m1, k2 tog, k5.

Row 6: K7, p20, turn.

Row 7: Sl 1, k17, k2 tog, m1, k7.

Row 8: K8, p19, k4.

Row 9: Sl 1, k20, k2 tog, m1, k4, m1, k2 tog, m3, k1, inc 1 in last st.

Row 10: K4, p1, k8, p18, turn.

Row 11: Sl 1, p15, k2 tog, m1, k4, *m1, k2 tog*, repeat *-* to last 5 sts, k5.

Row 12: Cast off 2 sts, k32.

Row 13: Sl 1, k3, p15, k2 tog, m1, k4, *m1, k2 tog*, repeat *-* twice, m3, k1, inc 1 in last st.

Row 14: K4, p1, k28, turn.

Row 15: Sl 1, p13, k2 tog, m1, k4, *m1, k2 tog*, repeat *-* 3 times, k5.

Row 16: Cast off 2 sts, k34.

Row 17: Sl 1, k3, p13, k2 tog, m1, k4, *m1, k2 tog*, repeat *-* 4 times, m3, k1, inc 1 in last st.

Row 18: K4, p1, k30, turn.

Row 19: Sl 1, p11, k2 tog, m1, k4, *m1, k2 tog*, repeat *-* 5 times, k5.

Row 20: Cast off 2 sts, k36.

Row 21: Sl 1, k14, k2 tog, m1, k4, *m1, k2 tog*, repeat *-* 6 times, m3, k1, inc 1 in last st.

Row 22: K4, p1, k20, p12, turn.

Row 23: Sl 1, k9, k2 tog, m1, k4, *m1, k2 tog*, repeat *-* 7 times, k5.

Row 24: Cast off 2 sts, k23, p11, k4.

Row 25: Sl 1, k5, *m1, k2 tog*, repeat *-* twice, m1, k3 tog, m1, k4, (m1, k2 tog) 8 times, m3, k1, inc 1 in last st.

Row 26: K4, p1, k23, p11, turn.

Row 27: Sl 1, k10, m1, k2 tog, k2, k2 tog, *m1, k2 tog*, repeat *-* 7 times, k6.

Row 28: Cast off 3 sts, k22, p12, k4.

Row 29: Sl 1, k15, m1, k2 tog, k2, k2 tog, *m1, k2 tog*, repeat *-* 6 times, m3, k2 tog, inc 1 in last st.

Row 30: K4, p1, k19, p13, turn.

Row 31: Sl 1, p12, m1, k2 tog, k2, k2 tog, *m1, k2 tog*, repeat *-* 5 times, k6.

Row 32: Cast off 3 sts, k36.

Row 33: Sl 1, k3, p14, m1, k2 tog, k2, k2 tog, *m1, k2 tog*, repeat *-* 4 times, m3, k2 tog, inc 1 in last st.

Row 34: K4, p1, k30, turn.

Row 35: Sl 1, p14, m1, k2 tog, k2, k2 tog, *m1, k2 tog*, repeat *-* 3 times, k6.

Row 36: Cast off 3 sts, k34.

Row 37: Sl 1, k3, p16, m1, k2 tog, k2, k2 tog, *m1, k2 tog*, repeat *-* twice, m3, k2 tog, inc 1 in last st.

Row 38: K4, p1, k28, turn.

Row 39: Sl 1, p16, m1, k2 tog, k2, k2 tog, (m1, k2 tog) twice, k6.

Row 40: Cast off 3 sts, k32.

Repeat Rows 1-40 until length desired. Cast off.

CONTINENTAL PILLOWS

Cast on 1 st and k1, p1, k1 into this st.

Row 1: (M1, k1) 3 times.

Row 2: M1, k1, p3, k2.

Row 3: M1, k3, m1, k1, m1, k3.

Row 4: M1, k2, p5, k3.

Row 5: M1, k5, m1, k1, m1, k5.

Row 6: M1, k3, p7, k4.

Row 7: M1, k7, m1, k1, m1, k7.

Row 8: M1, k4, p9, k5.

Row 9: M1, k9, m1, k1, m1, k9.

Row 10: M1, k5, p11, k6.

Row 11: M1, k11, m1, k1, m1, k11.

Row 12: M1, k6, p13, k7.

Row 13: M1, k13, m1, k1, m1, k13.

Row 14: M1, k7, p15, k8.

Row 15: M1, k8, k2 tog, k11, sl 1, k1, psso, k8.

Row 16: M1, k8, p13, k9.

Row 17: M1, k9, k2 tog, k9, sl 1, k1, psso, k9.

Row 18: M1, k9, p11, k10.

Row 19: M1, k10, k2 tog, k7, sl 1, k1, psso, k10.

Row 20: M1, k10, p9, k11.

Row 21: M1, k11, k2 tog, k5, sl 1, k1, psso, k11.

Row 22: M1, k11, p7, k12.

Row 23: M1, k12, k2 tog, k3, sl 1, k1, psso, k12.

Row 24: M1, k12, p5, k13.

Row 25: M1, k13, k2 tog, k1, sl 1, k1, psso, k13.

Row 26: M1, k13, p3, k14.

Row 27: M1, k14, sl 1, k2 tog, psso, k14.

Row 28: M1, p30.

Row 29: M1, k2 tog, k1, *(m1, k1) twice, sl 1, k1, psso, k1, k2 tog, k1 *, repeat *-* twice, m1, k1, m1, k2 tog, k1.

Row 30: M1, p32.

Row 31: M1, k2 tog, k1, *m1, k3, m1, k1, sl 1, k2 tog, psso, k1 *, repeat *-* twice, m1, k3, m1, k2 tog, k1.

Row 32: M1, p34.

Row 33: M1, k4, k2 tog, k1, m1, k1, *m1, k1, sl 1, k1, psso, k1, k2 tog, k1, m1, k1, *, repeat *-* twice, m1, k2 tog, k1.

Row 34: M1, p36.

Row 35: M1, k2, *m1, k1, sl 1, k2 tog, psso, k1, m1, k3*, repeat *-* 3 times, m1, k2 tog, k1.
Row 36: M1, p38.
Row 37: M1, k4, k2 tog, k1, *(m1, k1) twice, sl 1, k1, psso, k1, k2 tog, k1 *, repeat *-* twice, (m1, k1) twice, sl 1, k1, psso, k4.
Row 38: M1, p40.
Row 39: M1, k4, k2 tog, k1, *m1, k3, m1, k1, sl 1, k2 tog, psso, k1 *, repeat *-* twice, m1, k3, m1, k1, sl 1, k2 tog, psso, k3.
Row 40: M1, p41.
Row 41: M1, p42.
Row 42: M1, k43.
Row 43: M1, p44.
Cast off.
Rows 1–43 form one section of pillow. Repeat 3 times. Join together to form square.

The tiny pillows are edged with fancy lace, worked thus:
Cast on 4 sts.
Row 1: Sl 1, k1, m2, k2.
Row 2: K3, p1, k2.
Row 3: Sl 1, k5.
Row 4: K6.
Row 5: Sl 1, k1, m2, k2 tog, m2, k2.
Row 6: K3, (p1, k2) twice.
Row 7: Sl 1, k8.
Row 8: Cast off 5 sts, k3.
Repeat Rows 1–8 until the lace is long enough to go around the square, with ample fullness at corners.
Make pillow insert approx. 3'' (8 cm) square. Attach knitting with tiny sts or, if preferred, use the knitted square as a pillow sham. The continental pillows can be filled with lavender or potpourri to keep the doll's bedding fragrant and free from moths.

BEDSPREAD

Work Rows 1–28 of the Continental Pillow pattern. Cast off. Make 3 more and join together with tiny stitches to form square motif. Work as many squares as necessary to make the bedspread the size required, sewing them together neatly.

Harebell Edging (page 75) makes a neat finish to the bedspread. Allow ample fullness at corners. Embroider a simple flower at each corner of the squares, and in the corners of the pillows. The sheets on this tiny bed are fine muslin with feather-stitched hems. The little pillows match the sheets. Blankets are knitted in fine wool in the Crow's Foot Pattern (see page 82).

Blankets

Crow's Foot, Purse Stitch, Mock Turkish Stitch—all traditional patterns.
Use 3-ply cotton or wool and 2 mm needles for the blankets. The number of stitches will depend on the bed size. Test to ascertain the number of sts required, casting on enough to ensure a generous tuck-in. Bind with ribbon or use a picot cast-off.

CROW'S FOOT

Cast on any number of sts that can be divided by 3 to make the width required.
Row 1: Purl.
Row 2: M1, sl 1, k2, psso the 2 knitted sts, repeat to end of row.
Repeat Rows 1–2 until length desired. Cast off after purl row.

PURSE STITCH

Cast on multiples of 2, plus 2 stitches, to width required.
Row 1: K1, *m1, p2 tog, repeat from * to last st, k1.
Repeat this row until length desired.
Cast off.

MOCK TURKISH STITCH

Cast on multiples of 2 to width required.
Row 1: K1, *m1, k2 tog, repeat from * to last st, k1.
Repeat this row until length desired.
Cast off.

Blankets can be bound with blanket binding or a picot cast-off can be used to finish the edges.

Laces for Dolls' Bedlinen

Kate displays a pile of hemstitched linen sheets ready to be lace-edged, and a choice of three laces. From left to right they are One and All, in DMC 100 Cotton, double eyelet edging in DMC 80 Cotton, and rosebud edging in DMC 20 Cotton. Use the finest needles and threads you can find to create lace of gossamer fineness.
Kate is wearing the Blythe collar (page 42) as a yoke. The pattern for the pillows appears on page 80.

Row 3: K3, m1, p2 tog, k2, k2 tog, m2, k2 tog, k7, m1, p2 tog, k6.
Row 4: K6, m1, p2 tog, k9, p1, k3, m1, p2 tog, k3.
Row 5: K3, m1, p2 tog, k2 tog, m2, (k2 tog) twice, m2, k2 tog, k5, m1, p2 tog, k2, m2, k2 tog, m2, k2.
Row 6: K3, p1, k2, p1, k2, m1, p2 tog, k7, p1, k3, p1, k1, m1, p2 tog, k3.
Row 7: K3, m1, p2 tog, k2, k2 tog, m2, (k2 tog) twice, m2, k2 tog, k3, m1, p2 tog, k9.
Row 8: K9, m1, p2 tog, k5, p1, k3, p1, k3, m1, p2 tog, k3.
Row 9: K3, m1, p2 tog, k2 tog, m2, (k2 tog) twice, m2, (k2 tog) twice, m2, k2 tog, k1, m1, p2 tog, k2, (m2, k2 tog) 3 times, k1.
Row 10: K3, p1, (k2, p1) twice, k2, m1, p2 tog, (k3, p1) 3 times, k1, m1, p2 tog, k3.
Row 11: K3, m1, p2 tog, k2, k2 tog, m2, (k2 tog) twice, m2, k2 tog, k3, m1, p2 tog, k12.
Row 12: K3, k2 tog, k7, m1, p2 tog, k5, p1, k3, p1, k3, m1, p2 tog, k3.
Row 13: K3, m1, p2 tog, k2 tog, m2, (k2 tog) twice, m2, k2 tog, k5, m1, p2 tog, k2, m2, (k2 tog, m2) 3 times, k2 tog, k1.
Row 14: K3, p1, (k2, p1) 3 times, k2, m1, p2 tog, k7, p1, k3, p1, k1, m1, p2 tog, k3.
Row 15: K3, m1, p2 tog, k2, k2 tog, m2, k2 tog, k7, m1, p2 tog, k15.
Row 16: (K3, k2 tog) twice, k5, m1, p2 tog, k9, p1, k3, m1, p2 tog, k3.
Row 17: K3, m1, p2 tog, k2 tog, m2, k2 tog, k9, m1, p2 tog, k2, (m2, k2 tog) 5 times, k1.
Row 18: K3, p1, (k2, p1) 4 times, k2, m1, p2 tog, k11, p1, k1, m1, p2 tog, k3.
Row 19: K3, m1, p2 tog, k13, m1, p2 tog, k18.
Row 20: Cast off 13 sts, k4, m1, p2 tog, k13, m1, p2 tog, k3.
Repeat Rows 1–20 until length desired. Cast off.

ONE AND ALL EDGING

Cast on 25 sts.
Row 1: K3, m1, p2 tog, k2 tog, m2, k2 tog, k9, m1, p2 tog, k2, m2, k2 tog, k1.
Row 2: K3, p1, k2, m1, p2 tog, k11, p1, k1, m1, p2 tog, k3.

DOUBLE EYELET EDGING

Cast on 31 sts.
Row 1: Sl 1, k1, k2 tog, m2, k2 tog, k1, (m1, k2 tog) twice, k2 tog, m2, k2 tog, k1, m2, k2 tog, (m1, k2 tog) 6 times, k1.
Row 2: K15, p1, k3, p1, k8, p1, k3.
Row 3: Sl 1, k6, (m1, k2 tog) twice, k5, m2, k2 tog, (m1, k2 tog) 6 times, m1, k2.
Row 4: Cast off 3 sts, k13, p1, k16.
Repeat Rows 1-4 until length desired. Cast off.

ROSEBUD EDGING

Cast on 8 sts.
Row 1: M1, k2 tog, k1, m1, k2 tog, k1, m1, k2.
Row 2: M1, k2 tog, k4, m1, k2 tog, k1.
Row 3: M1, k2 tog, k1, m1, k2 tog, k2, m1, k2.
Row 4: M1, k2 tog, k5, m1, k2 tog, k1.
Row 5: M1, k2 tog, k1, m1, k2 tog, k3, m1, k2.
Row 6: M1, k2 tog, k6, m1, k2 tog, k1.
Row 7: M1, k2 tog, k1, m1, k2 tog, k4, m1, k2.
Row 8: M1, k2 tog, k7, m1, k2 tog, k1.
Row 9: M1, k2 tog, k1, m1, k2 tog, k5, m1, k2.
Row 10: M1, k2 tog, k8, m1, k2 tog, k1.
Row 11: M1, k2 tog, k1, m1, k2 tog, k6, m1, k2.
Row 12: M1, k2 tog, k9, m1, k2 tog, k1.
Row 13: M1, k2 tog, k1, m1, k2 tog, k4, k2 tog, m1, k2 tog, k1.
Row 14: M1, k2 tog, k8, m1, k2 tog, k1.
Row 15: M1, k2 tog, k1, m1, k2 tog, k3, k2 tog, m1, k2 tog, k1.
Row 16: M1, k2 tog, k7, m1, k2 tog, k1.
Row 17: M1, k2 tog, k1, m1, k2 tog, k2, k2 tog, m1, k2 tog, k1.
Row 18: M1, k2 tog, k6, m1, k2 tog, k1.
Row 19: M1, k2 tog, k1, m1, k2 tog, k1, k2 tog, m1, k2 tog, k1.
Row 20: M1, k2 tog, k5, m1, k2 tog, k1.
Row 21: M1, k2 tog, k1, m1, (k2 tog) twice, m1, k2 tog, k1.
Row 22: M1, k2 tog, k4, m1, k2 tog, k1.
Row 23: M1, k2 tog, k1, m1, (k2 tog) twice, k2.
Row 24: M1, k2 tog, k3, m1, k2 tog, k1.
Repeat Rows 1-24 until length desired. Cast off.

Bibliography

De Dillmont, Thérèse: *Encyclopedia of Needlework,* DMC Publication, Mulhouse, France 1924.

Klickman, Flora: *The Modern Knitting Book*, published by The Girl's Own and Woman's Magazine, London 1914.

Mrs Leach's Fancy Work Basket, R.S. Cartwright, London, 1887.

Needlecraft Practical Journals, W. Briggs & Co. Ltd, 34 Cannon Street, Manchester, *c.* 1911–1930.

Rutt, Richard, The Rt. Rev: *A History of Hand Knitting*, B.T. Batsford Ltd, London 1987.

Sibbald and Souter, *Dainty Work for Busy Fingers*, S.W. Partridge and Co. Ltd, London 1915.

Thomas, Mary: *Mary Thomas's Book of Knitting Patterns*, Hodder and Stoughton Ltd, London 1985.

Weldon's Practical Knitter, series published by Weldon Ltd, The Strand, London, *c.* 1890–1911.

Wright, Mary: *Cornish Guernseys and Knit Frocks*, Alison Hodges, Cornwall 1979.

Wright, Mary: *Granny's Lace Knitting and Great Granny's Lace Knitting*, self published 1986.

Zimmerman, Elizabeth: *Knitters' Almanac*, Dover, New York 1981.

Knitting Around, Schoolhouse Press, Pittsville, Wisconsin 1989.

Guilds

The Knitters' Guild of New South Wales Inc. can help you pursue your craft. For details contact the Honorary Secretary:
Knitters' Guild of New South Wales Inc.
72 Bettington Road
Dundas NSW 2117 Australia

The British Knitting and Crochet Guild welcomes new members. The Guild promotes both crafts and publishes the informative booklet *Slipknot*. For membership details contact:
Membership Secretary
Anne Budworth
228 Chester Road North
Kidderminster
Worcestershire DY10 ITH
Great Britain

Suppliers and Doll Studios

Australia

DMC Needlecraft Pty Ltd
51–55 Carrington Road
Marrickville NSW 2204
(02) 559 3088

Queanbeyan Cottage Crafts
Millhouse Gallery
49 Collett Street
Queanbeyan NSW 2620
(062) 99 2011

The Sewing Spot
Shop 7, Crawford Centre
Crawford Street
Queanbeyan NSW 2620
(062) 97 1695

Fyshwick Antique Centre
77 Wollongong Street
Fyshwick ACT 2609
(062) 80 4541

Dunbar Cottage Gallery
80 MacQuoid Street
Queanbeyan NSW 2620
(062) 99 4198

Florrie Allan Dolly Bits
P.O. Box 420
Kalamunda WA 6076
(09) 454 7681
*(Mail order service;
catalogue available;
fine needles.)*

Country Classics
(Antiques and Interiors)
Shop 1, Palmerston Lane
Manuka ACT 2603
(062) 48 7035

The White Birch
Shop 7
Manuka Village ACT 2603
(062) 95 9609

Living in Style
Shop 4, Style Arcade
Manuka ACT 2603
(062) 95 6894

Champion Textiles
16 O'Connell Street
Newtown NSW 2042
(02) 519 6677
(Mail order service.)

Blithe Bébés Dollmaking Studio
61 Dundas Court
Phillip ACT 2606
(062) 85 4276

Ellen Watt Studio
25 Graham Place
Queanbeyan NSW 2620
(062) 97 7346

Ria Warke 'The Doll Works'
71 Leichhardt Street
Kingston ACT 2604
(062) 95 0695

Kaye Wiggs, Doll Maker
18 Carter Crescent
Calwell ACT 2905
(062) 92 5968

Jan Clements, Dollcarver
19 High Street
Yackandandah Vic. 3749
(060) 27 1320

Tessa B Knits
98 Norma Road
Myaree WA 6154
(09) 330 3433

Cockington Green Miniature Village
Gold Creek Road
Gungahlin ACT 2617
(062) 30 2273

For information on heirloom
lingerie (page 59) contact:
Rose White Designs
P.O. Box 13
Kippax ACT 2615

Sindle & Loom
83 Longueville Road
Longueville NSW 2066
(02) 428 4995

Knit 'n' Spin
225 Rowe Street
Eastwood NSW 2122
(02) 874 1963

Anne's Glory Box
60–62 Beaumont Street
Hamilton NSW 2302
(049) 61 6016

Nancraft
247 Dorset Road
Boronia Vic. 3155
(03) 762 1751

Mary's Handcrafts
58 Queen Street
Ulverstone Tas. 7315
(004) 25 5988

Ceramic & Craft Centre
52 Wecker Road
Mansfield Qld 4122
(07) 343 7377
(Fine needles.)

Bramber Cottage
Hume Highway
Berrima NSW 2577
(048) 77 1235

United Kingdom

The Dollshouse Draper
P.O. Box 128
Lightcliffe
Halifax
West Yorkshire HX3 8RN

Vast selection of haberdashery for miniature dolls, minute ribbons, buttons, trims, hatstraw etc. Dress patterns for doll's house dolls. Good range of cotton print and pure silk dress material for miniature and larger dolls. Miniature knitting supplies for outfits for doll's house dolls, knitting patterns, needles, wool etc; tiny buckles to trim.

Catalogue and price list.

Nicola
Joan Nerini
20 Court Close
Patcham
Brighton
East Sussex BN1 8YG

Paper patterns for dolls' outfits to fit both antique and reproduction dolls 8'' to 30'' tall. Also patterns for Teddy Bears' clothes.

Excellent range of haberdashery including DMC thread suitable for knitting or crochet for dolls in wide range of colours. Very fine sewing needles, crochet hooks, miniature hooks and press fasteners, fine sewing thread, narrowest elastic. Finest knitting needles sizes 16–20 for miniature knitting. Knitting patterns for dolls' socks, gaiters and mittens.

Catalogue, leaflets and price list.

Doli Shoes
Gwendoline Longman
39 Welling Way
Welling
Kent DA16 2RL

High quality leather shoes and boots made to measure especially for your dolls, both antique and reproduction. Numerous styles and various colours available.

Catalogue and price list.

The Dolls House Emporium
Tudor Models Limited
Victoria Road
Ripley
Derbyshire DE5 3YD

Fantastic high quality dolls' houses for collectors and children, ready made or in kit form. Superb doll's house furniture and accessories. Excellent range of building supplies for making dolls' houses; also garden supplies. Exquisite range of miniatures for dolls' houses. Various doll's house families including bisque; also miniature Teddy Bear family for doll's house inhabitants.

Colour catalogue and price list.

Leominster Dolls Hospital
J. & Co. Mansell
1 The Gatehouse
Church Street
Leominster
Herefordshire HR6 8NE

All types of dolls repaired, antique and modern. Dolls' clothes repaired and restored too.

Postal customers only. Callers strictly by appointment.

Village Fabrics
30 Goldsmith's Lane
Wallingford
Oxfordshire OX10 0DN

Importers of top quality cotton fabrics, an extensive range of miniature prints for doll's house furnishings and clothes for doll's house dolls, also suitable for dressing larger dolls.

Dozens of samples sent on request and price list.

Fred Aldous Ltd
P.O. Box 135
37 Lever Street
Manchester 1 M60 1UX

Suppliers of handicraft materials including doll and toy making, knitting, lacemaking, embroidery and crochet. Good range of metallic threads. Have dolls, dolls' hair etc; also books.

Catalogue and price list.

Sunday Dolls
Sue Atkinson
7 Park Drive
East Sheen
London SW14 8RB

Make superb exclusive bisque doll's house dolls in 1/12th scale with 75 different faces to choose from. Also some 1/24th scale. All exquisitely dressed in elaborate period costume (the Rolls Royce of doll's house dolls). Also available—1/12th scale patterns for dressing doll's house dolls in period costume.

Colour catalogue and price list.

Dryad Specialist Crafts Ltd
P.O. Box 247
Leicester LE1 9QS

Fantastic range for all types of craftwork—lacemaking, embroidery, pottery, modelling, kilns etc. Balsa wood for doll's house enthusiasts. Equipment for designing and printing your own fabric for dressing dolls. Small print fabrics for patchwork—suitable for doll's clothes. Pins, needles, wide range of scissors plus threads. Many specialist crafts catered for.

Colour catalogue and price list.

The Lilian Middleton Doll Company
Days Stable
Sheep Street
Stow on the Wold
Gloucestershire GL54 1AA

Makers of fine bisque dolls. Range of items for doll collectors and enthusiasts including bisque doll kits and spare parts, eyes, elastic, clothing, shoes, socks, patterns and books. Dolls' houses, furniture and accessories.

Catalogue and price list of reproduction dolls only.

Hobby's
Knight's Hill Square
London SE27 0HH

Everything for the doll's house collector and restorer. Elaborate dolls' houses in kit form; also miniature shops, range of 1/12th scale wallpapers and accessories, extensive range of doll's house lighting, plus panelling, paving, doors, windows, cladding, bricks, stained glass—all materials needed for making dolls' houses and doll's house plans. 1/12th furniture kits, Turkish carpets, ready made curtains, chinaware, flowers and plants; also furniture plans.

Bisque doll's house dolls, also kits and vinyl flexible dolls, modern doll's house, furniture, fittings. Soft toy accessories and kits, plans for children's toys. Books on doll's house building, making miniatures.

Catalogue and price list.

Pick 'N' Choose—The Craft People
56 Station Road
Northwich
Cheshire CW9 5RB

All crafts catered for. Dolls, kits, heads, wigs, hats. Materials for dressing dolls, patterns, trimmings, all types of sewing threads, needlework accessories, lace-making and crochet equipment. Miniature baskets. Books on lacemaking, crochet, embroidery, smocking etc.

Catalogue and price list.

The Singing Tree
69 New King's Road
London SW6

1/12th scale exquisite dolls' houses, doll's house kits, furniture and accessories. Superb collectors items. Many items exclusive to The Singing Tree.

Catalogue and price list.

RECOLLECT STUDIOS
The Old School
London Road
Sayers Common
West Sussex BN6 9HX

Everything for the doll restorer and doll maker. Trade and retail suppliers. Quality reproduction bisque dolls and kits of all sizes. All types doll bodies, limbs, eyes, teeth, wigs, eyelashes, domes etc. Body patterns, sewing patterns for costuming old or reproduction dolls. Knitting patterns for dolls, including doll's house dolls. Doll stands, shoes, socks, hats etc. Wax doll's house doll kits. All items needed for doll and Teddy Bear repairs. Teddy Bear kits and clothes patterns, miniature ware for doll's houses, doll's house dolls and kits. Moulds, porcelain slip, kilns, tools, paints etc. for making bisque dolls. Books on dolls and Teddy Bears. Doll making courses.

Catalogue and price lists.

The Handicraft Shop
Northgate
Canterbury
Kent CT1 1BE

Dolls' wigs, hats, shoes, soft body fillings, stringing elastic, doll stands, mohair for wigs, eyes, parasols, miniature baskets and cradles. Dolls for craftwork, heads, limbs and mask faces. Vast range of everything needed for many types of craftwork.

Catalogue and price list.

Index